Praise for *The Effective Hiring Manager*

"Throughout my career as an army officer, C-suite executive and board member, I have used oral book reports as an effective method to both develop and synchronize the people I work with. *The Effective Hiring Manager* is not only a must read it will be our next group 'book.' The book reinforces everything that is critical to our firm. Don't just do things without thinking, do things that really matter and DO THEM RIGHT."

—John Hoffman,
Chairman and CEO, Pivotal Systems

"Mark and the Manager Tools team changed my life. They gave me the foundational skills I now rely on to be a good manager. *The Effective Hiring Manager* is another great example of this. If you want to make great hires, you've got to read this book."

—Ryan Carson,
CEO & Founder, Treehouse

"As with *The Effective Manager*, Mark Horstman strikes gold with practical guidance that can be immediately applied to the most consequential job of a manager—hiring the best people. This book will dramatically change how you view the hiring process and how you do it."

—Joseph D'Alessandro,
Deputy Chief of Grant Compliance and
Fiscal Services. School District of Philadelphia

"If you are serious about raising the professional talent standard in your organization, *The Effective Hiring Manager* should become your official hiring handbook. Every manager should get a copy, absorb the process and then implement the disciplines in the book. Read this, distribute this, practice this, and watch the change take hold."

"On Capitol Hill hiring mistakes are not just HR problems, they can also be political nightmares. Mark takes the mystery out of the hiring process by laying out a step-by-step process and anticipating challenges and resistance to change. You can't achieve your objectives and retain the best people if you don't hire the best people in the first place."

"This book is a wonderful, practical book for all managers. Do not hire just because someone leaves—think about it first. You may have just reduced your costs for free. Get your team to think about what they can stop doing—creative abandonment. A must read for all the managers on my team."

"Whether you are a seasoned leader or a first-time manager, with the advice in *The Effective Hiring Manager*, you will make better hires that strengthen your company. Mark Horstman provides practical guidance for each step of the hiring process."

THE
EFFECTIVE
Hiring
MANAGER

MARK HORSTMAN

THE
EFFECTIVE
Hiring
MANAGER

WILEY

For general information on our other products and services or for technical support, please contact our Customer Care Department within the United States at (800) 762-2974, outside the United States at (317) 572-3993 or fax (317) 572-4002.

Wiley publishes in a variety of print and electronic formats and by print-on-demand. Some material included with standard print versions of this book may not be included in e-books or in print-on-demand. If this book refers to media such as a CD or DVD that is not included in the version you purchased, you may download this material at http://booksupport.wiley.com. For more information about Wiley products, visit www.wiley.com.

Library of Congress Cataloging-in-Publication Data:

ISBN 9781119574323 (Hardcover)

ISBN 9781119574361 (ePDF)

ISBN 9781119574347 (ePub)

Cover image: © LPETTET/iStockphoto

Cover design: Wiley

Printed in the United States of America

V10013080_081619

This is what I tell my friends.

Every Manager Effective. Every Professional Productive.

Dedicated to the Manager Tools community: millions of listeners, all over the world.

Contents

Introduction

Hiring is the most important managerial practice.

THE PURPOSE OF THIS BOOK is to help you become an effective hiring manager. Effective hiring is the most important contribution a manager makes to his or her organization.

Great CEOs are often quoted as spending as much as 30% of their time on people. How are individual managers and executives doing with their responsibilities? Who's "ready now" for more responsibility? Who will be "ready next"? Who needs different responsibilities? Who is at risk for leaving the firm? Who, external to the firm, may be worthy of recruitment or a relationship?

With all that CEOs have to do—strategy, customer relations, governmental relations, investor relations, structure, finances, internal and external communications—most will say that the area they spend most of their time on is people. Despite the cynicism that accompanies the phrase, "People are our most important asset," CEO behavior tells us that it's true—even if the rank and file often don't feel that way.

CEOs do so because they have learned that every organization's engine of success is its talent: people. It's people who create, manage, and improve upon all the systems, processes, and policies that those people use to generate growth, revenue, profit, mission accomplishment.

In the long run, it's people that make the difference. Every result in every organization comes from people. It's not algorithms, or equipment, or software, or proprietary trading models, or cost leadership, or high quality that drives success—it's people.

Those ideas and systems are important, but people create them. Great people create great systems and processes and results. We here at Manager Tools often say that great people can overcome messy systems and processes to still produce great results. But if an organization's talent isn't great, there is no amount of great systems that will help average performers create great results.

If an organization's people are the engine of its success, then the decisions made about which people join the organization are the most important decisions the organization makes. And those decisions are not made at the top; they're made by individual managers.

My previous book, *The Effective Manager*, dealt with managing the people you already have. "Managing," in common usage, typically means the stuff we managers do day to day, with the people we already have. But that's because we do those managerial things on a daily basis. Hiring, though, most of us do pretty rarely.

And this is where our danger lies.

On our popular Manager Tools podcast, I've coined a phrase for tasks managers are responsible for that are both important and rarely practiced: *The Horstman Christmas Rule*. If you're someone who celebrates the Christmas season, the festivities are important to you. You look forward to it. Yet, when it's all over, you're wiped-out, tired, stressed out, and happy to have a few days off to recover.

That's because Christmas is important, but it only happens once a year. *We don't get better very fast at things we do rarely.* We're often stuck doing those things poorly and repeatedly.

Hiring is the most important thing we do, but we don't do it that often. That's not good.

Think about your organization when it goes through the difficult process of a layoff. It's bad enough that the concept itself causes fear throughout the organization and your team. Then it gets worse during the process: poor communication, messy mistakes, clumsy meetings, and often, poor decisions. The beginning of the great movie about Wall Street, *Margin Call,* shows this exceptionally well.

You know why layoffs are so often messy? Because most managers are going through a layoff for the first time. And even if they've done it before, it's been so long since the last one they don't remember what they told themselves never to forget.

Hiring follows the Christmas Rule. We don't do it often and it's important. Hiring well is ensuring that the most important asset of your organization, its people, are of the highest standard you can expect.

Imagine treating hiring in the opposite way, as a necessary but trivial task. You're super busy on some really important projects, and you really just need one person who has a specific skill.

You find someone; you interview him. You have doubts, and there are areas that will need watching. But he does have the right skills. You don't have a lot of time, and this isn't your biggest priority so you pull the trigger.

Unfortunately, your fears are realized. His attitude is poison to your team, he's thin-skinned, not collaborative, and because he knows he's necessary, he's arrogant about his value. After the fourth or fifth incident that your boss finds out about, she takes you aside and says, "What the heck were you doing hiring this guy?"

Seriously, what are you going to say? Are you going to mumble, "I know, I know, but I really needed someone"? That will get you a quick, "Well, now you got him," from a frustrated boss.

Or maybe she'll go big picture, and give you some critical career advice. "This is a serious miss. Hiring mistakes are nearly unforgiveable. Hiring poorly sends a message that you can't set and meet a high standard on the most important thing you're going to do for this organization long term. I gotta tell you, when we sit around and evaluate managers at your level, lack of ability to hire is a serious impediment to career growth."

And you'd be *lucky* if she did say it, because whether she says it or not, that's what she's thinking.

Or maybe it's your first hire, and you're likely to get a little leeway. Most managers say they could have used a lot of help when they first hired. And yet, there's probably not a lot of detailed help available in your organization. Maybe HR can tell you some things—but that's just about the process *they* use. It won't be about what questions to ask, or how to set up an interview day, or how to get your people together to talk about candidates after a day of interviews. They'll probably tell you that you'll want to schedule a panel interview, which are popular . . . and completely refuted as an effective technique.

Because hiring is so important, and so rarely practiced, we all need a clear, evidence-based, documented process on how to hire. Step by step. In detail. That's what this book does.

When you follow the guidance in this book, you'll become an Effective Hiring Manager.

About Manager Tools

My firm, which I co-own with my outstanding business partner Michael Auzenne, is a management consulting and training firm. We coach and train managers and executives at firms all around the world. In 2019, we will provide all-day training sessions to over 1,000 managers at our corporate clients worldwide. We also host training conferences all over the world, where individual managers can be trained. We will conduct over 100 of these training events in 2019.

However, if your company cannot afford to send you to training (we do offer a discount if you want to pay yourself), *almost all of the guidance in this book is available for free in our podcast, Manager Tools*. You can find the podcast on iTunes and at www.manager -tools.com.

As of this writing, our podcasts are downloaded about three million times a month, in virtually every country in the world. We've won many Podcast Awards over the years, thanks to our loyal audience.

Our podcast is free because the mission of our firm is to make every manager in the world effective. Many of them can't afford to buy this book.

Periodically, we will encourage you to go to our website for more guidance. We can't put all the podcasts in here—there are, at the time of this publishing, close to 1,000 of them. You'll see many instances of *There's a Cast for That*™ throughout this book. They are links to additional free content in our podcasts on our website.

A Note About Data

For the past 25 years, we've been testing various managerial behaviors and tools, to see which work and which don't. I used to hate it when the manager training I received, or the books I read, basically were filled with someone's opinions, or they proffered an idea and then used a few anecdotes to support their position. We at Manager Tools like the aphorism, "The plural of anecdote is not data."

We have tested and refined all of the recommendations given in this book. We have viewed thousands of interviews, and tested all of the major recommendations here on population samples that give us high confidence about our recommendations.

That being said, no study can completely predict how any one manager's hiring will be affected by the tools we recommend. Every situation is different. Often, that's what many managers say when they come to us for help and explain their situation: "My situation is special/different/unique."

Almost always, it's not different at all. But because there's a chance that a manager's situation *is* unique, we will tell you this: *Our guidance is for 90 percent of managers, 90 percent of the time.*

It's possible that you're in a special situation, but I doubt it.

A Note About Gender

You'll notice that, throughout this book, we will use different genders for managers—sometimes male and sometimes female. All of our content at Manager Tools—all of the audio guidance in podcasts and all the shownotes—use a nearly perfect balance of male and female examples.

The reason for using different genders for managers is that all of our data show that men and women make equally good hiring managers and, for that matter, executives. If you're a female hiring manager, we're glad you're reading this book, and we're here to help.

Let's get started.

SECTION

1

Principles

1

The First Principle of Effective Hiring—Don't Hire

WHEN YOU FIRST THINK YOU might need to hire, think again.

You don't have to hire immediately when you have an opening. The strategic-thinking Effective Manager considers other options first. That's how your CEO wants you to think.

Most managers, when they learn about an opening on their team or are overloaded with work, immediately start thinking about asking for permission to hire. We're consumed with approval and process thoughts.

The average manager just naturally assumes that when someone leaves, you hire someone else. But that's one of the ill-considered ideas that drives executive leaders crazy. To an executive, there's nothing wrong with hiring someone . . . but there is something very wrong with hiring reflexively.

If you work for a smart director [manager of managers], she's going to ask you a few questions when you ask for permission to hire.

"Did you consider not filling the job?" *No.* [Huh??]

"Why not?"

This exchange does not make this manager seem like a creative thinker, or a manager who thinks about his role in the organization.

This manager is thinking about himself, but the director is thinking: he's not a big picture guy. He's just a cog in the system, doing his job. Low likelihood of upward potential.

To an executive, an opening is not "a spot that has to be filled." To a leader, it's a cost savings in the form of less salary. You read that right. It's an opportunity to be creative. It's an opportunity to reexamine the work that's being done, and who's doing it. Maybe there's a way to get the really important work done without hiring. Maybe we can agree to let some things go and get everyone focused on what really matters.

And no, this is not the time to invoke some hackneyed idea of rapacious executives always expecting fewer and fewer people to do more and more. Yes, that happens, but it is rare. It's just reported a lot because it's dramatic. As managers, our first responsibility is to the organization, not to our team. So our first steps should be to get what the organization wants.

Going and asking for hiring approval right away—first—is backwards. Hiring approval will be granted more readily to the manager who can show that he has done the proper due diligence on the work, its value, people, and costs—before he asks to open a requisition.

So let's start with assuming we can't fill the slot. That "they" won't let us. In other words, if you couldn't get approval, how would you solve THAT problem? The problem is no longer the request to hire, and sourcing, and screening, and interviewing. The problem is how to get the most out of those you have, because whom you have is all you have.

Not being able to hire happens all the time, of course . . . but everybody forgets that too easily. Openings happen during layoffs and downturns. In those times, authority to hire is routinely denied.

A manager who assumes her first action is to hire, because her "problem" is "not enough people all of a sudden," may not feel terribly creative about solving the other problem: what's the right way to do our job with the people we HAVE. Because, if the problem really IS not enough people for the work, the work becomes a static force, an immovable object.

So to avoid wasting time thinking about what we can't have, we assume we will NOT get anyone new. These are the new parameters to our problem and talking to our boss or to HR has nothing to do with them.

If you can't fill the slot, there are two broad areas to consider: get more work out of the existing team or figure out what work not to do. And the most likely solution includes some of each.

We assume we have all the people we're going to get. There are "fewer people now" to do "the same amount of work." That means either that (a) people are going to simply take on the additional work, adding more hours or being more efficient and/or (b) some of the work being done is going to no longer get done.

Think for a moment about a manager with five directs. Assume that compensation is 50% of his operating budget (a general rule of thumb). So the loss of one person—all things being equal, which they never are (ATBEWTNA)—is a savings of 10% of budget. This is a serious savings.

Any manager who was presented the opportunity to "figure out which work to cut back on so that you could cut your budget by 10%," would jump at the opportunity.

That means some work not getting done. And this is your opportunity to think like a leader. And the best way to get to what's not going to get done is to follow our guidance for Delegating to the Floor.

How to Solve a Hiring Problem Without Hiring

First, ask your directs to prioritize their work. Ask them to analyze their work based on its value and priority to the organization (them, you, the division, the firm). Tell them to make a list of everything they're working on and roughly how much time it takes, and then to rank it not by hours but by value. It shouldn't be more than 20 things, we would guess. If it is, there are going to be a lot of things that take VERY few minutes, and those are probably things that won't be missed.

It might sound like this: "Here's what I'd like you to do. Spend an hour, today and/or tomorrow. Make a list of everything, or nearly everything, that you're working on. You can look at your calendar, your piles of work, etc., anything you can think of to help you. I'm not going to wait, though, for a week, for you to do a time diary of everything you touch in the next week. That's probably overkill.

"Then, list all your work in order of importance, and next to each item you're working on, put down the amount of time it takes you each week. It's okay to estimate."

Don't be surprised if they submit something that says they work 80 hours a week. That's wrong, and it does NOT prove that they're working feverishly at home. It means they don't really know how long they spend on things. That's okay. The point here is that pretty quickly among the items in their lists there will be a drop off in time spent and in value delivered.

Next, ask your directs for a recommendation *from them* about what won't get done. After you've asked them to create the lists, ask them further to review the lists, think about them, and determine what on those lists could afford to not be done.

Here's how it might sound: "Once you've got your list, review it. Analyze it a bit for me. And come back to me with a recommendation for what work you could get away with not doing, assuming a bunch of new, higher priority work was coming your way. Think about the time you could save, simply not doing some stuff. That's what I want: a list, with recommendations on it of stuff you could set aside."

Consider their recommendation, and then make the decision yourself. It's important you ask for a recommendation, and NOT a decision. That way, they won't feel as much risk about the analysis. It might sound like this: "Ultimately, I'm going to make the decision. If you'll do the analysis, I'll likely follow your recommendation. But this way, I'm responsible. As you get better and more confident at this, I'll start letting you make the decisions as well, and I'll still be responsible."

Then ask them to direct questions to you. The last stage is that, after you make the decision, they stop working on those things they recommended and you decided. When they express concerns, tell them that all questions about what they're working on come to you. In other words, if they think someone is questioning why something that used to get done is NOT being done, they would tell that person to talk to you, the manager.

If you expect your directs to do the analysis and make the decision themselves, and then deal with the consequences, all at once, learning by trial by fire, they're not going to do what you ask. They're going to hide some work and/or try to get everything done, which is a complete contravention of the whole purpose of this effort.

Some caveats: this guidance is largely for managers of individual contributors. If you're a Director, managing managers, you don't have to make the decision for them, they can do it themselves. On the other hand, if you lose one of your managers, you may want to also consider reorganizing. It's not as easy as most companies make it out to be. But Directors have a great deal more leeway than they realize.

There are roles and teams where this kind of analysis is harder. For example, in a customer service contact center (a large bank's call center), representatives are unlikely to have a list of multiple tasks that have varying levels of value. Their primary role, serving customers by phone, is 90% of their time/value.

If that's you, you may quickly realize you can skip this step, but don't lose sight of how a manager thinks, because roles like this are the exception. Your next role may be different.

2

The Second Principle of Effective Hiring—Set Your Bar High

If you want to make managing easier, make hiring better.

WE BELIEVE THAT THE MOST serious organizational weakness in modern organizations is hiring poorly. *Companies and managers routinely hire far below the quality we could find, largely because we don't set standards, we don't train, we don't have measured processes, and we don't improve.*

Our organizations have systems to test the quality of raw materials coming in to our plants. We reject anything that is even a *little* out of tolerance. We have nondestructive testing methods for inbound materials, and for our own manufacturing processes. We have financial standards for investing capital that are incredibly rigorous—and monstrously difficult to prepare for at times. We have rigid standards for expense reporting.

And then, for the most important decisions organizations make—who will work here—we have no formal, communicated standards. Managers are usually not required to go to training. There usually isn't any approved interview training. If there is either of these, it's under the auspices of Human Resources. It's likely much more about legalities than effective decision making. Of course we need to know what questions *not* to ask. But that will only help us not be sued. It won't help us make excellent hiring decisions. [If you're young and at a company that provides good interviewing training, don't make the mistake of assuming that that's true everywhere. It's true almost nowhere. Count yourself lucky, and take advantage of it.]

In the worst cases, we leave the decision to some senior manager who's never been trained, never been given feedback, has never been assessed on her true positive and true negatives, is never held accountable, and mostly goes with her gut. We've tested more than 20 seasoned managers we've met over the years who had the reputation for making good gut decisions on hiring. We have never found a single case where they notably outpaced the results of other managers, based on looking at records of true and false positives and negatives.

Hiring without high standards is like trying to make a gorgeous wedding cake substituting raw wheat for flour, while adhering to every other step in the process. The problem with that analogy, though, is no one would eat the cake, because it wouldn't become a "cake." But with bad hiring, we end up eating the cake day after day after day of working with our new hire, the poor choice.

We managers make our pain by hiring poorly. We hire poorly, then we complain about our workload because the very people we hired don't turn out to be as good as they "should" be. They create more managerial work for us, and reduce the time we have available for the projects we think will move our part of our organization forward.

If you feel like you're always putting out fires, don't forget in your systemic solution to change those you're hiring by raising your hiring standards.

Bad hiring is the root cause of so many *other* downstream issues: performance, retention, succession planning, productivity, and profitability.

Say you hire the wrong person, or not even the "wrong" person, just someone who doesn't scale as well as you'd like. And because the person doesn't scale, you can't give her a team to manage when workload expands. But you need to get more work out of the group she's in. Because your poor hire can't get *more* out of the group you already have, *you have to hire more people. And when you hire more people to do work that your competitor does with fewer people, your competitor is more productive and therefore usually more profitable than you.* You're not going to be the market leader if your entire organization is continually repeating the mistake of hiring folks who aren't good enough now or won't be good enough to grow with the organization.

All of the above is why *if we do decide to hire,* our first thought must be to set the hiring bar *high.*

Before we ever start interviewing, our guiding principle must be to avoid hiring anyone who has the slightest chance of being a hiring mistake. We *want* the reputation in our industry, and among candidates, that "it's not easy to get hired there."

Managers complain to us regularly that they have to go through hundreds of résumés, and it's time-consuming. [We'll explain how to screen résumés later.] Why waste time looking at lots of résumés that are sure to be "no's"? You'll start with a smaller pile if you raise your hiring standards, because lots of candidates won't apply, because "several of my friends have interviewed there and didn't get an offer."

Tell people in your industry that you have high hiring standards. Tell them that your hiring process is designed to reduce your risk. Tell them that if it's close, it will probably be a no. Plenty of those who listen will shy away. And those whom you would say no to are hanging around others whom you would also say no to.

But good candidates *won't* shy away. Good candidates will actually be drawn toward your opportunities. They'll know that a high bar for hiring means that the folks you already have are good. They'll know they won't be the only top performer on the team. They won't be Harrison Bergeron, weighted down with rules and processes built to minimize the damage of weak performers, rather than giving top performers opportunities to excel.

And there's an internal benefit, too. Telling your existing team that the bar is high *protects them*. Tell them: "You folks are good, and I won't hire just anybody to work alongside you."

Now your team won't shy away from saying no to someone they have doubts about. They won't just say yes because they heard that one of the candidates is your favorite. They won't just say yes to an interviewee because they're desperate for help.

They'll start looking for reasons to say "no" in an interview. They'll be looking for areas to be concerned about. Which is why we interview anyway. If you're looking for reasons to say yes, you'll find them. But it's the reasons we should have said no that come back to haunt us.

And we want them looking for problems. If they're interviewing someone who will be a peer, a big part of their thinking is having help with their workload. But we managers have to know a bigger truth: ***The only thing worse than an open position is filling it with the wrong person.***

Ask any manager who has ever made a bad hire. They'll tell you: never again.

3

The First Principle of Effective Interviewing—Say No

So we've determined that we have to hire, after figuring out ways to prioritize work among remaining staff. And we've committed to setting a high bar. As we move to the interviewing phase of the hiring process, our guiding principle is simple: ***Look for reasons to say no.***

The best way to demonstrate the rationale for this is by using a matrix that we popularized at the Manager Tools Effective Hiring Manager Conferences (Figure 3.1). We conduct these publicly all over the United States and overseas, and privately for clients as well.

	Don't Hire	Hire
Fit		
No Fit		

Figure 3.1   Hiring Matrix

The matrix is a classic 2x2, showing the choices we have in interviewing and the possible outcomes. Our *decisions* are shown as two *columns*—either we hire, the rightmost column, or we don't—the left column. The *outcomes* are shown as rows. A good fit—someone who turns out to be a good hire once he's on board—is the top row. And a bad fit—someone who turns out poorly—in the bottom row.

The first lesson in the matrix is a simple one: it's not necessarily true that someone is a fit just because we hire her. *We only know whether someone is a good hire **after** she has been performing in the role.* Most managers mistakenly conflate "saying yes" with a good fit: "If I like him, then he's right." But that's not always true.

This leads us to important hiring guidance: effective hiring is based on *outcomes*, and not on *decisions*.

You'll notice the red arrow above the right, "Hire" column. That's where most managers are focused during the process. They *want* to hire. That opening *needs* to be filled. You've probably felt this way yourself—we have.

That right column "hire" mindset is important to understanding why *the purpose of an effective interview is to find reasons to say no.*

Let's just walk through the matrix's various outcomes to further understand manager decisions and hiring outcomes. Obviously, what we want is to hire someone who is a fit: the top right cell (Figure 3.2).

	Don't Hire	Hire
Fit		**GREAT!**
No Fit		

Figure 3.2   A true positive outcome

This is what is known as a "true positive." Our decision to hire ends up being supported by good performance once the candidate is part of our team.

That desire makes it easy to think that our job in interviewing is to "hire." It may be more accurate to think of our decision as "offer" as opposed to "hire." Whether our offer is accepted or not is out of our control. It would be a little weird to hope to say yes to someone in an interview and then not hire him. We have to assume *while we're interviewing* that any offer will mean a hire.

The next possible outcome is that someone is a fit, but we say no, and decide not to make an offer. This is the outcome in the top left cell (see Figure 3.3). An outcome like this is called a "false negative." [We said no, but the person "should" have been a "yes."]

It's disappointing or worse to a manager who is thinking of hiring. "We missed a good candidate! As desperate as we are, we can't afford that!" This is the kind of thinking that leads to lax hiring standards, *which often comes as a direct result of thinking that the purpose of interviewing is to find reasons to hire.*

Fortunately for our sanity, most of us don't track candidates' success in other roles after we turn them down.

	Don't Hire	Hire
Fit	Disappointing	**GREAT!**
No Fit		

Figure 3.3 A false negative outcome

If we interview someone and choose not to make an offer, and the person would not have been a good fit, that's what is known as a "true negative" (Figure 3.4). It's represented in the bottom left cell. That's a good outcome—we did our job and didn't hire someone who wasn't right.

	Don't Hire	Hire
Fit	Disappointing	**GREAT!**
No Fit	Good	

Figure 3.4   A true negative outcome

But now we come to the most important cell in the matrix: the bottom right. This is the case where we have decided to offer/hire someone, *and the person ends up not becoming effective.* He or she does not turn out to be a good performer. This is what is known as a "false positive" (Figure 3.5). We said yes, but we should have said no.

	Don't Hire	Hire
Fit	Kind of disappointing	**GREAT!**
No Fit	Good	**HELL ON EARTH**

Figure 3.5   A false positive outcome

Manager Tools affectionately calls this outcome, "Hell on Earth." The "Hell on Earth" hire is the employee who performs poorly or tears down your team. [There are two reasons to fire someone: failure to perform and not working well with others.] This hire will take too much of your time to manage. He will drag down the performance of your team. Hiring him will reflect poorly on you. One of the primary goals of this book is to help you avoid, at all costs, "Hell on Earth." If you're going through your first hiring experience as a manager, remember what we said earlier: *Ask any manager who has ever made a bad hire. They'll tell you:* **never again.**

Consider again the red arrow at the top right of the matrix. It highlights the "Hire" column. Because we want to "hire," we focus on "finding someone." We start looking for positives. And most candidates who have reached the final stages of interviewing *clearly have characteristics to recommend them.* When we combine our desire to hire with confirmation bias, our focus on our decision *increases the chances of a Hell on Earth hire.* What we're trying to do—hire—increases what we definitely do not want.

Now reconsider the red arrow at the bottom left of the matrix. It highlights the "No Fit" row. This is the right approach to hiring: **Eliminate any possibility of a bad outcome.** If we wipe those possibilities out (Figure 3.6), all we're left with is either the great

	Don't Hire	Hire
Fit	Kind of disappointing	**GREAT!**
No Fit		

Figure 3.6   Eliminate the possibility of a bad outcome

outcome of a true positive hire, or the disappointing outcome of a false negative.

So, I repeat: *the purpose of any interview is to find a reason to say no. To eliminate all candidates who would not be a fit.* What we're left with is either exactly what we want, or a small disappointment.

When effective hiring managers interview, they're looking for problems. They're not looking for strengths. If you start looking for strengths, you'll find them. Everybody has them, including the Hell on Earth hire.

The default answer when interviewing must be "no." If "no" is our default, then that's what you say if you have doubts at the end of an interview. If your team conducts interviews of candidates (who want to become their peer), and they express doubts, say no to that candidate. [There are exceptions to this, which we'll talk about later.]

If you think more interviewing might reveal more positives to "balance out" the negatives, it's time to say no.

If you finish interviewing and find no problems, then and only then have you eliminated a bad fit. Then you can start thinking about hiring.

SECTION
2

Preparation

4

Behavioral Interviewing and Preparing Your Hiring Criteria

BEFORE WE CAN START INTERVIEWING, *we have to know what it is we're looking for*. That means analyzing our job for behaviors, and creating interview questions.

You may be inclined to skip this portion of our guidance because, "I already have my interview questions." Trust us—it is *unlikely* that the interview questions you are using are good enough, crisp enough, written down, in order, to meet our criteria of setting the bar high and an interview's purpose being to say no. Worst case, you'll only have to create a new set of questions once for each of your roles, and it will take 45 minutes each time—a worthwhile investment for the best interview you'll ever create.

Looking Beyond Traits and Characteristics

The keystone of effective interviews is having great interview questions. But how are great interview questions created? What do we want to know?

This is where most managers go wrong. They say, "Well, I want smart, hard-working, nice, ethical, knowledgeable . . ." While no

21

one can argue with such a conclusion, the problem here is that these traits and characteristics are insufficient.

We have to be careful about questions regarding personality traits or internal characteristics that we associate with this job's success. Why? While everyone who is good at the job has these traits and characteristics, *there are also some people who have the traits and characteristics who could not do the job.* That is, traits and characteristics may be necessary, but they are not sufficient.

So what questions do we ask to be sure that this person will be able to do this job?

It's the end of that question that matters: "*do* the job." To be a success at something, you have to be able to *do* it. Not think it, not smart it, not ethical it, not characteristic it. The bright hard nub of job success is *doing.*

The best way to see whether someone can do the job is to find out whether he's done it before.

But this makes us have to work a little bit harder. What we've done in this short analysis is make a synecdoche error: We've let the whole of the job obscure the tools that are used to do it. If we see only the job, the only way to be sure that someone *can do the job* is for someone to *already have done the job.* That conclusion creates succession and growth and talent market friction problems very quickly. Everybody would be stuck where they are.

So we dig a little deeper and ask, If we can't do a job for job comparison (which really isn't specific enough anyway), what can we look for to determine whether someone *can do the job?* Since you've followed along this far, you've probably figured it out: Jobs are so multifaceted that "doing the job" is too gross an analysis.

We don't just want traits and characteristics. That's not enough. On the other hand, it would be too restrictive to demand that someone had done the exact same job before. And so we come back to the word "doing." What do we mean?

Doing is a great word here, because it points us to *behavior.* Behaviors aren't traits or characteristics—they're (usually) traits or characteristics *put into action*. Don't our classic success phrases like *get the job done*, *make things happen*, *achieved*, and *got there* all imply *action* and *activity* beyond states of mind, or attitude, or traits, or characteristics?

What we are looking for in an interview is for someone to show us that he or she has engaged in the behaviors that we believe are necessary to do our job well.

Behaviors are the engines of doing. They are specific enough that they get past the too-general "job" idea. They are portable enough that if a candidate has engaged in them before it's reasonable to assume she can do them again. They are known, and they are measurable.

The best way to interview someone, then, is to look for behaviors that are necessary and sufficient for success in our role, and which the person has engaged in previously.

If you're still clinging to the idea of traits and characteristics, you're not alone. There's a classic concept called **hire for attitude, train for skill**. The idea is, figure out what attitudes you want, and then just make sure that you can train people on the skills you need them to do.

Unfortunately, this approach is flawed, for two reasons. First, you don't have enough time to train everyone on every skill needed for your job, and your company won't support it. We've got to screen for skills when we interview. Second (and this is my favorite part), *traits are only proven by behaviors which reveal them*.

Suppose I told you someone was smart. Nevertheless, you observed him regularly *do things* that you wouldn't characterize as "smart." At what point would you question how smart he is? The fact is, *"behaving with smarts" is what we mean by "smart." Behaving ethically is what we mean by ethical. Behaving with kindness is what we mean by kind.*

If you still want to hang on to the idea of attitudes and skill, think of it this way: Hire for behaviors that show the maximum skill and attitude.

Knowing the Necessary Behaviors for the Job

What we've just walked through is the analysis that leads us to behavioral interviewing. Once we realize that we have to look for behaviors, we are led to the core preparation question: **What behaviors are most important, necessary, and sufficient to do this job well?**

In order to get to those behaviors, we have to do two things: define what the behaviors are, and then analyze our role for the ones that matter.

Lucky for us, behaviors have already been well defined. In a professional context, there are five behaviors:

- **The words we say.** What actual words we utter verbally.
- **How we say those words.** The tone, speed, and volume of those words. Someone who says, "I'll do it" quietly and with hesitation is behaving differently from someone who says the same words quickly and more loudly.
- **Facial expressions.** If someone says "I'll do it" with a smile, that's different from someone who says so with a frown or a grimace.
- **Body language.** Someone who crosses his arms, rolls his eyes, and says, "I'll do it" is behaving differently than someone who says it leaning forward.
- **Work product.** There are several categories of work product:
  - **Quality.** How well the work is done against an overall standard.
  - **Quantity.** How much work is done.
  - **Accuracy.** Whether the work is done correctly, measured against known processes like language and math and processes.
  - **Timeliness.** How much time is taken to do the work, usually against a time standard like a deadline or a known measure.
  - **Documentation.** Any durable output reasonably associated with the work: emails, spreadsheets, letters, posts, images, reports, written statements.
  - **Safety.** Actions taken against known protocols or standards of risk reduction, often, though not always, physical.

This list is probably a lot to take in, but don't worry. Once you have that framework roughly in your head, you'll discover it's just a different way of looking at what you already know. Trust us that if you follow our job analysis process, you'll end up with behavioral questions that will frame the role you're hiring for in important, necessary, and sufficient behavioral questions.

Knowing now that we need to focus on behaviors, and knowing what they are, how can we identify the behaviors that are most important to the role for which we're hiring?

Luckily, it's not hard. There are four readily available sources for the kind of information you need:

- Job descriptions
- Performance reviews
- Top performers
- Manager Tools questionnaire

Job Descriptions

Job descriptions are sometimes good sources of information about a role. Too often, of course, they're out of date, or they don't even exist. Take whatever you can from the job description you have. Make a list of the skills, traits, abilities, and characteristics (STAC) that are listed or implied. Don't narrow the list you come up with— think of this phase of hiring as brainstorming, rather than deciding. Some managers who have listened to our guidance on this topic say they put an identifier next to each skill, trait, etc, to mark where it came from: JD—job description, TP—top performer, etc.

If there isn't a job description, again, don't worry. In our experience, performance reviews, asking questions of top performers, and our questionnaire are more valuable in most managers' cases. If your organization has good current job descriptions, count yourself lucky.

Performance Reviews

Next, take a look at recent performance reviews for directs who have held this position, or even one close to it. Look at all of the criteria on the review, both quantitative and qualitative. **What we mean by criteria are the various areas that are evaluated based on the form, not what was written about the person whose evaluation you're reviewing.**

Make a list of criteria that strike you as particularly important. Don't worry. Trust yourself, even if you're a new manager. There are no wrong answers, and you'll learn as you interview more and more.

For instance, maybe there's an evaluation of teamwork or team skills (surely there is). Perhaps that is particularly important to you because your team hasn't been working well together lately. Maybe there's another evaluation criteria about planning skills that seems important because your team has been inefficient lately, not having processes in place they can lean on when their workload spikes. Surely there's a criterion for technical skills. Perhaps your team isn't as strong as you'd like in those skills right now, due to the rapid change in technology happening in your area. Make some notes of those criteria. Consider making some comments about their relative importance to you/your team/your roles.

This area is an example of one of the biggest problems in management—managers doing nothing because they fear being "wrong." Managers look around and think, "Those managers 'over there' don't seem to be as uncertain as me. They seem to know what they're doing. Probably they've been *taught* all this stuff before."

Trust us: *Those managers haven't been taught all this stuff.* They don't "know." And they certainly don't know what the "right" answer is, because there almost never is one. Even Manager Tools guidance isn't the only way. It's just the only way presently available that has data to prove that it works. So make your best estimation, and keep going.

Remember—you're brainstorming right now, not cherry-picking. Write down anything that might be helpful. Add it to your list.

Top Performers

Next, take a look beyond the criteria to the actual comments and rankings and scores of the employee's reviews you've gathered. What scores seem especially important to you for the role? What comments matter most?

Now go one step further: Which qualitative comments give you insight comparing your best team members to those less effective and efficient? When you look at your best performers, what comments stand out? Is it that they achieve because of technical skills, or team work, or process development, or communication? Are your poor performers poor communicators? If they are, you may want to be careful of hiring a great technical talent who isn't a solid communicator. (In our work, poor communication is too often accepted in a strong technical candidate, leading to great frustration and poor teamwork in the future.)

All of that thinking gets added to your list. Now we're going to ask our top performers a few questions by email: What do *they* think makes them effective, and why? What STAC components matter the most to them?

You can do this one of two ways. You can send them your list (perhaps edited down a bit) and ask them to comment on it. It might look like this:

I'm gathering information to help us evaluate our upcoming hire. Below you'll find a list of things I've noted, looking at our job description and performance reviews. Would you please comment on any of the items that are particularly important to you? Which items do you think of as being indispensable, or nearly so, for our new team member? Also, if there are criteria that seem less important, let me know that as well. And if I've missed something, send those areas along too.

I'm not looking for a new job description now. I don't think this should take more than 20 minutes to review and comment on. I know you've got plenty to do. Also, please remember that you will be conducting interviews of any candidate who makes it to the final stage, so please contribute with that in mind.

Or if you think you'll get better results, just ask people to send their own lists, without sharing your list with them. You know your team best. Do they need something to start with? Most do. But maybe they have their own ideas and you know you can trust them. That email might look like this:

I'm gathering information to help us evaluate our upcoming hire, to help me create interview questions. Would you please take a few minutes to think about what skills, traits, abilities, or characteristics (STAC) make you particularly effective in your role? Why are you good at what you do?

I'm not looking for a new job description now. I don't think this should take more than 15 minutes. I know you've got plenty to do. Also, please remember that you will be conducting interviews of any candidate who makes it to the final stage so please contribute with that in mind.

You'll probably get your answers in 24 hours. Add them all to your list.

We don't recommend asking your weakest performers to respond. We've tested that, and found that it's not all that helpful. What your weaker performers list as important may be an indicator of their incorrect priorities in the role. We've also found a much higher likelihood of requests for resources and complaints about systems in their analyses. *You've set your bar high and are trying to find more top performers. Focus on them.*

Manager Tools Simple Questionnaire

Our last readily available source of information is a simple question-naire for any role that we've prepared and refined over the years. You can fill it out fairly quickly. If you like, you could also ask your top performers to do so. (Some of it will be repetitive for them, after sending the email request described above.)

It's as simple as filling in the blanks.

- The reason the company created this job:

  _____

  _____

- The most important ways a person doing this job should spend their time:

  _____

  _____

- The two or three most important duties of this job are:

  _____

  _____

- What this job takes to be successful is:

  _____

  _____

- The simplest, easiest way to see whether this job is being done well is:

  _____

  _____

- If I followed high performers around for a day, what I would see them do:

  _____

  _____

- Work product the person produces that I report on to the organization:

  _____

  _____

- What my top performer does that makes her so good:

  _____

  _____

- The one or two metrics that this team lives and dies on are:

  _____

  _____

What you have now is a pile of information. Review it. What's critical? What's important but less so? What may not be important enough to screen for? What's relatively unimportant? Make notes. Maybe all you'll do is highlight the critical factors.

Now, with all the behavioral raw material you've gathered, it's time to create the interview questions you'll ask.

5

Creating Behavioral Interview Questions

Now that you know the behaviors that are most important, it's time to develop behavioral interview questions that will allow you to assess candidates against them.

The most effective interview technique in the world today is to use behavioral interview questions. There are reams of data on the technique, comparing it to others. Until there's a new way (AI, perhaps), you can't call yourself a good or professional interviewer unless you're asking behavioral questions.

The best example of behavioral interviewing today surprises many managers. It's software developers being asked to write code or debug some code during a technical interview. While most of us don't think of this as a behavioral interview, it is. It proceeds from the same premise: Past behavior is the best predictor of future behavior. If the primary behavior in the role is writing code, and you can actually assess that behavior, why wouldn't you?

The same would apply to a role where using spreadsheets was a key factor. There are wide disparities in how people assess their own skills. Some people consider themselves experts in MS Excel, for instance, but can't create a pivot table. Why not assess their behavior? We have heard surely a hundred anecdotes of managers doing so and finding "experts" who stare at some relatively simple Excel problem and can't even begin to solve it.

This is not to say that every role lends itself to such a test. It is to make the point that such a test *is in fact a form of a behavioral interview*. Past behavior/performance is the best predictor of future behavior, and in these cases, objective skills can be behaviorally "tested."

Of course, it's not possible* to "test" someone's ability, for instance, to get a team aligned and fully communicate over a several-month project. So we *ask questions about past examples* of the behaviors we are looking for rather than *directly testing them*.

You've probably heard or experienced some of the other formats and types of questions that are asked in interviews. Almost all of them are worthless *because they are terrible predictors of true positives and true negatives*.

- Asking, for instance, hypothetical questions: "What would you do if . . ." This only gives the candidate a chance to hazard what is likely a very good guess at what the right answer is.
- Asking intellectually challenging questions: "How many ping pong balls can fit in a modern passenger airplane?" This has been popular of late (but mainly because it makes interesting news and some of the companies who use it are of interest to many).

---

* Some companies attempt to re-create such skills by using exercises, often as part of an "Assessment Center." These can work, but are almost always a company-wide program, involving HR and perhaps an entire department to run the simulations with volunteers and various exercises lasting usually a whole day. An individual manager can't replicate this.

But they're not useful questions unless the role requires such estimation and problem solving on short notice. And while there are such roles (management consulting, for instance), it's unlikely yours is one of them.

Even the classic question, "Tell me about a weakness/Tell me your greatest weakness," isn't all that useful, according to interview results and performance comparisons. While it does get to self-awareness, that's usually something easily determined by asking a number of behavioral questions. What's more, high performance comes from leveraging strengths, not from improving someone's weaknesses. Also, sadly, most interviewees aren't terribly truthful with their answers.

"Unstructured" interviews have become more popular. They are also equally terrible at predicting performance. This is where the candidate asks all of the questions. They're certainly easier for the interviewer to prepare for, and maybe even more "fun" for the interviewer. But that's irrelevant. What matters in interviewing is efficient prediction of future performance.

There's another "type" of interview that can be called "unstructured." This is the interview conducted by the unprepared interviewer. This is just an unprofessional way to go about doing the most important strategic job of managers: assessing talent. It's funny that those who conduct these interviews reject other ways because the *other* ways don't have "data" to support them. Maybe funny is too kind a characterization.

If you're a manager who tends to be analytical and you're looking for data to support whatever managerial/professional approaches you take: *In my more than 30 years of interviewing candidates all over the world, there has never been any system that has any significant predictive effectiveness other than behavioral interviewing.*

How a Simple Behavioral Interview Question SOUNDS

A good behavioral question has three parts: the helpful lead-in, an open-ended beginning, and the behavior you're looking for. Put it all together, and it sounds like this:

- "Sometimes we have to provide service to a difficult person. Tell me about a time when you served someone whom others might have described as difficult."
- "We manage a great deal of data and systems relied upon by other departments. Describe a situation when it's been necessary for you to create and maintain data accurately. What did you do to ensure the data began and remained accurate?"
- "This role deals with a lot of details that together make a big difference. Describe a situation when you noticed a particularly important detail and had to alert others to its importance."
- "You have to think broadly to achieve in this role. Describe a situation when you had to work to consider all relevant information, even some that others might have not valued, to make a better decision."

Each of these questions has three parts. It's the use of the three-step building process that makes creating a behavioral interview question simple.

The Three Parts of a Simple Behavioral Interview Question—And Why

We've already shown the three parts: the lead, the question, and the behavior. Before we describe how to build the overall question, it helps to explain *why* the parts are important to the question.

Part 1 is the lead. It's often skipped, but it's there for a *big* reason. The lead tells the candidate exactly what we're going to expect in the job. We're *telegraphing* what we're looking for. We're making it easy, *but only for those who have what we're looking for. We can telegraph what we're expecting a candidate to do in the job because if he hasn't done it, it will be obvious when we probe any answer that isn't based on direct and related experience.*

Frankly, we **want** to make it easy for those who have the experiences we want. When decisions are tough, the decision support method ought to "spread the field": make the worst performer as far from the best as we can get them.

Part 2, the question itself, asks for an expansive answer. Note that in our example question we're making a request rather than asking a question: "Tell me about a time when . . ." You don't want to start with a who or a what or a why, generally. Those are certainly good question words for many interview questions, but generally **not** for behavioral questions. Behavioral interview questions suggest the need for a narrative, a description, a longer answer than most candidates tend to deliver to who/what/why questions.

Part 3, the behavior part of the question, is closely related to the lead. In the lead, we give the candidates an idea of what our job will require them to do. In the behavior part, at the end, we state specifically what we're looking for from their answers. It's couched in the form of a situation. What's interesting about this is that many candidates don't hear the behavior. They've heard the lead, they think they can just talk about a recent experience that matches what we've shared, and they either don't choose well or don't have what we're looking for.

But that's okay, because if they don't have it, we want to know that, and if they *do* have it but don't highlight it, we'll be probing their answers to see whether it's there.

How to Create Part 1: The Lead

There are really two parts to creating the Lead. The first is thinking about the key activities that you expect in this role. The second is actually crafting the wording, which is pretty easy.

For the first part, the activities we expect from the role, use the raw material from your earlier research. Further, here are some questions to ask yourself:

- If I followed each of them around for a day, what would I see them do?
- What reports do they provide me about their work, and what do those reports suggest they are doing?
- What work product do they produce that I report on to the organization?
- What does my top performer do that makes her so good?
- What are the one or two metrics that this team lives and dies with, and what activities do they require?

This gives you is a whole lot of "stuff"—they might not exactly be behaviors, but that's okay. It might be "stuff" like "runs project meetings," "produces C++ code for our core application," "inspects bridges and compares them to published standards," or "creates new product ideas."

The other way to do this is even easier—ask your directs to answer the questions. You have to change the questions to their point of view, but that's easy enough. And by the way, give them no more than 48 hours to do it. We've found that all the good work happens right in the beginning.

Now for crafting the wording. Simply put the "stuff"—the behaviors, if you've been that precise—into a lead-in statement, a stand-alone sentence, with an introductory phrase that approximates, "Periodically we engage in behaviors in this area here." Some examples:

- "We often are required to come up with new product ideas."
- "Sometimes we have to recommend quality initiatives with a lengthy presentation."

- "Frequently we're asked to deliver product to customers within narrow delivery timelines."
- "We routinely have to persuade customers to think differently about pricing."

How to Create Part 2: The Question

This is the easiest part of all three. You can choose from a prepared list.

- Tell me about a time when you . . .
- Describe a situation where you . . .
- When have you had to . . .
- Walk me through an experience where you . . .
- Share with me an example of you demonstrating . . .
- Give me an example of a time when you . . .
- Give me an example of a situation where you . . .
- Think of some time when you . . .

There are more that you could use if you prefer. But don't spend too much time here: Spend less here and more time on knowing what behaviors matter in the job.

How to Create Part 3: The Behavior

Simply take those behaviors—that "stuff" from your preparatory work—and add it to the question that you started in part two.

Part one and part three are closely related. If you use the exact same words, it might seem funny to you, so change them a bit.

6

Behavioral Interview Question Examples

HERE ARE SOME EXAMPLES OF effective behavioral interview questions. They come directly from the Manager Tools Interview Creation Tool, available to licensees of our work. The Interview Creation Tool provides behavioral questions like these (as shown in the Appendix) for any manager to use to conduct highly effective behavioral interviews. It asks you a series of questions related to categories of successful behaviors in the role you're interviewing for, evaluates the relative importance of those categories, and creates an entire interview based on your preferences. It also gives you criteria to look for in both effective and poor answers.

If your new hire will have to give presentations as part of her job:

- You're going to have to present regularly about the status of your work to people beyond just our team. Describe a situation when you presented to a group and how you went about ensuring your presentation was effective.

For a direct who will be involved in multiple projects at the same time:

- None of us get to work on one thing at a time. Describe a situation when you have successfully managed multiple projects simultaneously.

For a manager:

- Managers here are expected to grow the skills of their team members. Describe a successful development effort for one of your directs that you created and managed over time.

For a manager where your company uses metrics:

- We use metrics here to track performance and communicate status. Tell me about some metrics that you created or applied to your team. What were they, how did you communicate them, and how did you report results?

SECTION

3

Screening

7

Screening Résumés

Now that we've thought carefully about our hiring standards and developed the interview questions that will serve as our hiring criteria, it's time to start looking at candidates.

If you've skipped our guidance on creating your hiring criteria and behavioral interview questions, be careful: *Without knowing what to look for, screening résumés is much harder.*

Screening résumés is your first step in whittling down the interested and potentially competent candidates into a manageable group to interview. We know lots of managers who screen résumés when they're doing other things, and consider it a chore.

This is a mistake. Hiring is important. Screening résumés is part of hiring. Doing something important while doing something else is galactically stupid.

Smart résumé screening saves you a lot of time later in your process. You'll know more about what to look for overall, and also more about each candidate who makes it through the screening.

Here's what to look for when you're screening résumés.

Titles—What to Look For

First things first: Look at the titles of jobs the candidate has had over his or her career. We're not looking for a successful career path at this point, but rather something much simpler: In our opinion, does this person appear to have done the kinds of jobs the right candidate—a true positive candidate—would have done to prepare for the role for which he or she is applying?

We say "appear" because there's a reasonable amount of variation in job titles, and in some cases, it's hard to tell, based on a title alone, whether *that* title (never having come across it before) means the same as *this other title* in which we have high confidence as a good indicator.

There are plenty of companies in which the "manager" title means someone without a budget (the standard is that someone called manager has a budget). There are places where the "manager" title doesn't connote responsibility for supervising and developing directs (despite its typical connotation of those aspects). There are places where the title "Director" doesn't mean "manager of managers," most notably in technology firms.

There's also the problem of title inflation at small firms (and even some bigger firms). The thinking goes, "The guy at the top of a billion-dollar revenue firm is called CEO, then if I'm the founder of my three-person start-up, I'm at the top, so I'm CEO, too."

As a general rule, the problem with small company title inflation is confusing the metrics of "close to the top" and "far from the bottom." This is a simplification, but to earn a true "C-Suite" title, one not only has to be at the top of a firm, but also far from the bottom. If there are only two layers in a firm, no one ought to be called "senior vice president" of anything, and there isn't a C-Suite, yet.

These vagaries of the title/job/career naming conventions help us learn an important lesson about screening résumés. It's important to note on this first of several guidelines that we are not building a series of hard logic "or" gates here, with any one "no" resulting in failure/elimination of the candidate. At the same time, this doesn't contradict the Manager Tools rule that the purpose of all pre-employment screening is to say no.

How is that possible? We are still *absolutely* looking for reasons to say no to candidates. The smart manager knows he is far better off ending up with not a single phone interview out of a pile of 20 résumés, all things being equal, than having 15 of those résumé holders scheduled to be screened. While it's possible that a pile of résumés was that good, it's unlikely, and 15 out of 20 being judged "good enough for a screen" would suggest *insufficient screening standards*. For an inexperienced hiring manager, unfortunately, this is compounded by the fact that *it gets harder to say no to candidates as the process progresses*.

But the reason there's no easy black-and-white test is the lack of standards for résumés, and the lack of similarity in industries and job titles, and norms and means for responsibilities, and nomenclature. We can't build a purely logical screening model when there is so much variability in the data (words on the résumés) available to us.

What we have done here is create a list not of black/white either/ors, but rather of data to which to apply your judgment. For job titles, it sounds like, "What do I think of these titles?" "How do I feel about the jobs this person has had?" "Are these the kinds of titles I would expect to see?" "Did others who have this role now have similar/identical job titles when they were considered for this role?"

That said, it would be completely reasonable to look at a series of job titles on a résumé, perhaps, say, from a different industry, be unsure of their significance, *and to use your lack of knowledge, and the lack of affirmative data, to decide to put this candidate's résumé in the "no" pile*.

And if you're thinking you don't have enough experience to have that judgment yet so you can make a good call, **believe us when we say yes you do**. Too many of us as managers always seem to be in competition with "the right way to do something, which probably a lot of people know but I don't." And this lack of knowing "the right way"—*which never really exists*—causes us not to trust ourselves. We spend far too much time second-guessing ourselves, taking too long, being uncertain, and taking halfhearted steps.

Rest assured: ***You have all the judgment and decision-making skills you need for the role you're in, right now.*** Yes, you'll have more and better judgment skills about screening and hiring later in your career than you do now. Yes, you'll look back and think, *Oh my, how did I ever keep any job back then, as little as I knew, and as often as I had to fake it while it felt like everyone else knew what was going on?*

But the fact that you don't have the judgment that comes from the greater experience you'll have later in your career is a tautology. Of course you don't, and nobody expects you to. *But you are still expected to exercise the judgment you do have and make the decisions that you're supposed to make, come hell or high water, good outcome or bad, regardless of your inner sense of unpreparedness.* Fear of failure is not an excuse for a manager to do nothing, or to take whatever steps you take timidly, without speed and purpose.

If you're new, one smart way to use that guidance when screening is to say, *"If I don't know, that means 'no.'"* Rather than sitting around wondering what something is/means, *and trying to determine whether it's good,* trust yourself that if you're managing people doing this job, you know the right kinds of jobs that someone should have. If someone doesn't have them, but you worry that the jobs they have had *might* be perfect substitutes, think again. Say no to the substitutes and move on.

This is only our first screening step. It's at the highest level. Don't automatically start looking deeper into job responsibilities if you don't like/understand the titles you're seeing. We are not trying to find what might make the candidate good for us! We're trying to rule him out.

If you have doubts, say no.

Dates—What to Look For

Now look at dates on the résumé: How long did the candidate hold the positions listed? Were there only three months in the job you really want her to have mastered, but over six years at a preparatory role that isn't considered terribly difficult at most firms?

We want more experience in the more valuable roles, when possible. We also want to take note of a classic detail mistake in résumés: listing only the years someone was in a role, versus the month and year. If someone lists a role as having been from 2002 to 2003, we don't know whether he held that role for two weeks or 24 months. A considerable discrepancy. Generally, an absence of the detail of months is an effort to hide short stints or unbalanced stays in certain roles. If it is two years, or even two months, it could be an ethical violation, and a no-brainer elimination.

We're going to recommend considering saying no if the candidate doesn't have any roles where she stayed more than a year. Repeated short stints in roles is a bad sign. There are exceptions, but remember: We're trying to rule people out.

We're also looking for recency of experience. Having had all of the right titles but having had them five years ago is a strike against a candidate. And this is often a one-strike game.

Believe it or not, we also see résumés without dates, which is an effort to obscure information that we need. Some candidates who have "too much" experience are told to leave dates off. But that's misleading. It may imply that lack of clarity and truthfulness, and a willingness to withhold reasonable amounts of information, is a reasonable approach to situations of disagreement.

The most likely dates to be absent are those accompanying education. This is typically done to avoid "age-ism": not hiring someone because of age. We all can do the math, subtracting a candidate's university graduation year from today's year and, making the assumption that someone graduated from university roughly at age 21, we can determine age.

Some candidates and recruiters use this logic: Because a date associated with my education might allow you to determine my age, and since for you to discriminate against me because of my age is unlawful, it is quite appropriate for me to not share that information with you. Their refrain is, "I don't *have* to include that I was fired from a job (they're right, they don't have to), and therefore I *will not*, to keep you from using that against me. That's the same as leaving off my graduation year to avoid unlawful discrimination."

But this is fallacious because choosing not to hire someone because he or she has been fired is completely reasonable and legal, while leaving off a graduation year presupposes an unlawful intent to discriminate.

If someone leaves out enough dates that you feel are reasonable to know, we recommend you say no not because of age (which you may well not be able to tell) but because he has deliberately obscured useful information. Not having enough positives in a résumé is as much a reason to say "no" as having plenty of negatives.

Finally, we're looking for gaps in employment history. The general rule regarding résumés is that even if a candidate is unemployed (for good or bad reasons), that period of time must be accounted for. Perhaps someone was taking care of a sick spouse or parent. Perhaps someone took a two-year sabbatical and didn't look for work and didn't have to. Even though the impetus for the sabbatical was being fired, perhaps, it's standard for candidates to cover the time period as if whatever he or she was doing was a job. "Jan 99—Mar 01: Caregiver" is a completely appropriate way for someone to account for utility during what could be a time period left unaccounted for.

When it comes to dates, there is a fine line between a résumé that is legitimately "persuasively truthful" and one that is inappropriately "truthfully persuasive." The former—the right way—starts with truth and attempts to make it as persuasive as possible.

The latter starts with a goal of persuasiveness, and attempts to fit truth—selectively, unclearly—into a persuasive narrative.

We have seen too many résumés whose authors can legitimately say, "there's nothing untrue there," and we were left with the conclusion that a candidate could not be trusted. Dates are often a way to make this decision.

Companies—What to Look For

Most managers look at jobs almost exclusively. But the same job title at two different companies can be quite different. Depending on the quality, size, industry, stability and growth of the firm, the candidate was responsible for bigger or smaller tasks, had to meet lower or higher quality standards, worked with more effective or less effective people, used systems like or different from yours, etc.

Some companies provide notably better experience than other companies. Experience with the best companies is two to three times better than with most others.

The question this raises, of course, is which companies are better than others, and why. For that there is no easy answer, but there are some general rules.

The first key to thinking about the company experience of a candidate is to *find out what you can about whom they worked for*. When you see a name of a firm that you don't know, don't assume that you can't learn information that is useful to your screening process. If you have a candidate in your maybe pile, find out about the companies you don't know about. Remember through all of this process, though, that you're not looking for reasons to rule someone *in*, but rather to rule someone out.

Certainly, for some more well-known companies, you have some general knowledge. And you can find public information about public companies. For some companies that are perhaps close competitors to you, you have some knowledge.

- Companies that are growing provide better experience than those that stay the same size. Growth generally means success. That means more responsibilities over time in the same role, which means learning and development. It means working with new, different people over time, which means increasing need for better people skills. When we say growth, we don't just mean number of people; on the contrary, we mean revenue and/or profit growth. The very best companies, when results improve, *do not* hire more people. They get more out of the ones they have, through productivity gains (which means everyone having to do more).

- This is not to say that working at a shrinking company is necessarily bad. *There's a Cast for That*™: *Downturn Rite of Passage*. Working at one or two companies for a stint while they go through a recession is not a problem and can be good experience.

- Keep in mind that growth for different-sized companies is different. For Wal-Mart, the largest company in the world, to grow 10%, they have to add the equivalent of a Fortune 50–sized company to their revenues in one year. That's impossible (without acquisitions). For a very small company, though, 10% is almost the minimum amount of growth they could achieve and say they're growing. It just gets harder to grow the bigger you get.

   But a small company that might be staying flat is worthy of some concern. No-growth small-company experience for a candidate often means all kinds of inefficient, internally focused behaviors they'll bring to you.

While there's no clear delineator between small and big companies, a good *rough* rule is about 100 employees. Those 100 employees at a company that doesn't think it's small have similar characteristics and tendencies to others with fewer than 100 folks. One hundred to 500 is a good rough estimate of medium-sized, and they are generally—*generally*—similar. Bigger than 500 is big. They usually have all the characteristics of the biggest companies.

Don't assume that if you're not growing you want to hire someone from someplace that isn't growing. All things being equal, you want someone from some organization that is growing.

If you're asking someone to make a move from a big to a small company, or vice versa, and that person only has experience in large organizations, that's a red flag. It's not a reason to rule someone out, but it is a reason to ask about the change in your interviews, if they progress to that stage.

Another good general rule is to take note, or at least have a concern, when someone is coming to you with significant changes in two corporate characteristics. If someone works in your industry but is in a big company and you're small, that might be fine. But if he is in a big company *and* in a different industry (with perhaps no experience in your industry), that presages a challenge.

One way to potentially mitigate this, if you decide to interview a candidate, is to make sure to ask about the systems he used in his previous roles. If someone is "close" for one of your roles, but has never used your systems, never worked with your technology, hasn't ever managed a budget . . . these kinds of operational disconnects can be a significant detractor to the person's early effectiveness. Make a note on his résumé to cover that if he is screened or comes in for a face to face interview.

Career Progression—What to Look For

When it comes to thinking about people's career paths, it's easy: Ask yourself: *Have they grown?* The key here is that there are different ways to grow.

If someone has been in basically similar roles for a number of years in one firm, look for increasing responsibilities within that role or significant learning based on industry/technical changes. It might be okay to stay in the same role, but we have to see increasing mastery of the skills needed, learning of new skills in that role, and leading/

teaching/mentoring of others in the role or around her. If those kinds of experiences aren't shown on the résumé, it's unlikely she has them.

Also, be wary of someone who has been in the same role in a number of different firms of roughly the same size. That's not only not growth, but it's potentially problematic in terms of loyalty and relationships.

An important generally accepted rule around career progression is never hire someone into a managerial role in your firm if she's never managed before. This doesn't mean you can't hire a manager from another company into a director role at yours. This is often done when smaller companies hire bigger company managers into director roles, because the scope of a manager's job at a bigger company is often much greater than the equivalent title at a smaller company.

But hiring an individual contributor from another firm to be a manager at your firm is almost never a good idea.

Responsibilities—What to Look For

Responsibilities usually make up the majority of résumés. The reason they do is because everyone has them. Every job has responsibilities, and they're relatively easy to find from job descriptions or performance reviews or the like. Responsibilities are the benign, unimportant, low-hanging fruit of résumé preparation.

Responsibilities are useful and even necessary to know. But there is a *huge* problem with scanning a résumé for responsibilities.

The first is that candidates often bullet-ize responsibilities. Bullets are reserved for accomplishments on effective résumés. Many candidates who put their responsibilities into bullet form know this and are attempting to turn their responsibilities into accomplishments. To an accomplished résumé screener, this suggests low performance.

Remember that someone who has been fired from a job had the exact same job responsibilities as someone who was a high achiever in the role. What this often means is that by bullet-izing an accomplishment, and slightly changing its wording, a candidate can imply—without stating—accomplishing something simply because he was given a responsibility.

This means that *we must be especially vigilant to read each bullet and separate those that are actual accomplishments from simply responsibilities.* A résumé that has bullet-ized responsibilities *and no accomplishments* is an enormous red flag. Assume this person has been fired from every job he's had, or that she is so bad at the job that you're still going to definitely want to say no.

Assuming we have a résumé with both responsibilities and accomplishments, our key task is *determining whether or not the responsibilities are commensurate with the role/title.*

Too many of us mistakenly assume that the responsibilities for any role can be safely assumed to be equivalent to those for whatever role we have ever known that shared that same title. But of course this is false, and it leads to a lack of vigilance regarding experience.

Experience isn't the jobs someone has had. Experience isn't even the responsibilities she's had. **Experience is the accomplishments she's achieved in her roles.** If you take a job title as a broad-brush equivalency for experience, you'll miss the situations where the responsibilities diverge from your assumptions. Sometimes that's good, and sometimes bad. But mostly bad.

For each job, take a critical eye to the job title. Assuming it's a job title about which you have some knowledge, consider what that job title means to you in terms of experience. Think about someone whom you've known who is good at that job. And then compare your sense of what that job title means to the responsibilities the candidate lists.

Don't assume. One of the biggest mistakes we make when interviewing is assuming that what a title or a role or an experience means where we work is the same everywhere else. But company size, company growth, quality of the organization, the manager, and technology all play a role in what a responsibility actually is and means.

A good example of responsibilities being assumed away is when we hire a manager. Lots of us mistakenly assume that manager roles are quite similar. But they're not. Some managers have three directs; some have 15. Some have to manage contractors; some don't. Some have to manage across multiple shifts; some don't. Some managers write performance reviews; some don't. Some managers have budgets; some don't. Some managers have clearly defined internal customers; some don't. Some managers have clearly defined goals; some don't. Some managers are required to create formal performance development plans; some aren't. Some managers manage projects; some don't. Some managers have to manage distant directs; some don't.

So for each job, ask yourself whether the responsibilities fit the title. Then ask whether or not the responsibilities are sufficient for that role relative to the role you are hiring the person for.

Also, look for *increasing* responsibilities over a candidate's career history. More experience (if only in the form of time) means that a good candidate would have increasing responsibilities within each job in addition to moving through higher levels of responsibility in different jobs. Increasing levels of responsibility in each job is especially important in someone whose role has remained relatively stable. A flat career relative to role without increasing responsibilities within that role suggests someone who won't change, or won't develop. That might be fine . . . but probably not.

It's not necessarily a concern that at some point a candidate took a step backwards in responsibility. That may be due to a move to a bigger company, or it could be a career setback. It might be a reason to rule him out; if you're uncertain, make a note to ask, if they survive this round of scrutiny.

Accomplishments—What to Look For

Ahhhh, accomplishments: the saffron of résumés. Accomplishments are the reason résumés exist, despite all evidence to the contrary. We have seen so many thousands of résumés with bulleted *responsibilities* we've gotten cynical about bullets. It used to be that bullets indicated accomplishments. Now even terminated candidates bullet-ize their résumés.

So it is no longer enough to look for bullets. Too many of us look at a résumé, know that accomplishments are typically indicated by bullets, *read a bullet-ized responsibility and call it an accomplishment, and we give credit where credit is not due*. When we see a manager do this, we worry not just because of the *tactic*, but also because it indicates a dangerous *strategy* of assuming in the positive, which is akin to looking for strengths. But résumé screening, of course, is all about saying "no." Creating the correct, and negative, *confirmation bias* is perhaps the most important mental aspect of résumé screening. And interviewing as well.

Here are some simple rules for screening accomplishments:

Is It an Accomplishment?

We want to screen out anything that could be a responsibility masquerading as an accomplishment. Sentences that start with "Responsible for . . ." are 99% likely to be a responsibility. Often managers will tell us, "no, they're trying to show that they were given more responsibilities than the standard person in this role." While this may be true, it's *very* unlikely (and much more indicative of a screener's confirmation bias problem).

If someone is a manager, do not assume that anything that starts with "Managed" is anything other than a responsibility. If someone did manage 15 people, and the role you're hiring for only requires eight, that's still not an accomplishment. Yes, it would be worth noting relative to responsibilities, but nothing more.

But this is also one of the best examples of the subtlety of looking at responsibilities and accomplishments on a résumé. Suppose someone had managed 15 people, and the managerial role for which you were screening him has eight direct reports. And previously in your firm some managers had struggled with moving from managing four directs to eight. So you're inclined to look at those 15 directs and "check a box" for managerial competence for this candidate.

But this is likely a wrong move. While number of people supervised *well* is an excellent accomplishment, "well" is an accomplishment to be delineated by exceeding some standard. Number of people supervised cannot be assumed to be in any way an accomplishment.

There are two primary reasons for this. First, you have no idea what the average span of control was at the firm where he was managing. Fifteen may be small where he was. And perhaps these were all directs doing identical work, while your role requires aggregation of work from different specialists. Typical average spans of control are larger when individual work is similar; smaller spans of control are more likely when work has to be aggregated to create value. *So span of control isn't easily compared across organizations.*

Second, *someone managing a certain (high) number of people who doesn't list specific accomplishments relative to that responsibility may actually be attempting to **hide** that she did **not** do the job well, because if she had, she would have listed specific accomplishments related to achieving high performance and retention.*

Is It a Noteworthy Accomplishment?

There are some accomplishments that are technically accomplishments but are roughly the equivalent of "damning with faint praise." Even if we learn to say no to résumés that have responsibilities disguised as accomplishments (because "this person is not accomplished"), we can still be swayed by one *with* accomplishments that aren't notable enough to suggest a top performer.

For instance, "Achieved quarterly goal of . . ." While it's always good to have achieved a goal, it's also true that someone who didn't achieve the goal would have been putting his job at risk. That means achieving a given goal simply means he was in the group that wasn't at risk for losing his job. Surely that's not the standard we were hoping our candidates would have met. To be an accomplishment worthy of note, it would include some indicator of uniqueness above and beyond simply achieving the role's set standards.

Meeting the standards of a job isn't very much of an accomplishment. Words like, "Only one" or "Top 10%" or "Number 1" or "President's Circle" (assuming that can be qualified) are indicators that someone was a "relative out-performer." Look for special qualifiers to separate excellence from keeping one's job.

Is It an Unmeasurable Accomplishment?

Many résumés are filled with accomplishments that are unmeasurable. They make it sound as if the candidate did well. But to an accomplished résumé screener, too many of these leave a bad taste.

- *Example:* "Noted for." There is a big difference between a boss saying one day, "That was good," and that same boss describing a specific result on an annual performance review as "something which set her apart." *Both examples could correctly be cited as "noted for," but only one is exceptional in the screening process.*
- *Example:* "significant." Sometimes achievements are significant. You know it when you read about it. "Number one" certainly qualifies. "Best" is good (though not as good as number one). But without some other qualifier, "significant" isn't always so. In fact, to an experienced résumé screener, using the word significant without any other qualifiers that would then make "significant" redundant is a red flag of likely accomplishment inflation.

Another word to look for similar to "significant" is "important." If something is important, *the importance should be prima facie*. To have to name something as important, significant, notable, or worthy almost surely proves it wasn't. To say, "Noted for significant performance as NBA All Star in 2016" is redundant. "NBA All-Star in 2016" is sufficient to capture the accomplishment. Adding the qualifiers detracts from the quantification.

Qualification without quantification is inherently suspect to a résumé screener looking at accomplishments.

And if you need further convincing, read this accomplishment and ask yourself what you truly *know* about how good it is:

- Noted for significant contribution to department's quarterly performance.

An exception to vigilance relative to qualified accomplishments is when they are used as a part of a résumé that includes an equal or greater number of quantified and exceptional accomplishments. The quantification shows the level of excellence and gives the qualified assertions added credibility.

And yes, it's true that someone unskilled in résumé creation could have had an inestimable career and clumsiness will obscure it. But remember two things: We're looking for reasons to rule people out, and we're not evaluating the person, we're evaluating her résumé.

Finally, if you'll start looking for these soft, unmeasurable, unquantified "accomplishments," they will start jumping out at you. You'll move to the next level of screening mastery. You'll probably also recall many résumés of previous candidates you allowed to be interviewed for which you'd love to have "do-overs." Welcome to the club.

Education—What to Look For

The value of screening for in the area of educational history diminishes as a candidate develops professional experience. That only makes sense, in that professional accomplishments are much more likely to be predictive of future *professional* accomplishments than educational accomplishments would be.

But for a more junior professional, effective educational screening is *essential*, and it is still necessary for many senior candidates.

Ask three questions when thinking about a candidate's education:

- Is the educational level sufficient?
- What was the quality level of the education?
- How did he perform during his education?

Is the Educational Level Sufficient?

The answer to this question starts with the role you're recruiting for. Some roles require no education beyond compulsory levels. Some require university level. Some require still more. If a candidate doesn't have the necessary education, put the résumé in the no pile.

But it isn't necessary to stop with the level of education that is *required* for the role. A smart hiring manager asks herself whether or not her most effective performers in the role she's looking for have that level of education, *or perhaps even higher*. (As a general rule, you'll want to consider level of education *at the time someone took over the role*.) If we're looking for reasons to say no, it would be a reasonable additional screen to go through your "maybe" pile and create "no's" out of those candidates who passed the "necessary" test but didn't pass the "higher education/higher performer" test.

As we examine a candidate's educational background, though, we must remember *the most common mistake in educational screening: thinking that someone finished when he or she did not*. The most common place for this mistake to occur is in time spent at a college or university. A hiring manager sees a listing such as, "Los Angeles College, Finance, 1997–2001," and thinks that this candidate *graduated*. But experienced recruiters and managers would tell you he did not. The candidate has listed the four years—usually associated with the time it takes to earn a degree—and what he studied—akin to a major. But there is no assertion here that the candidate received a degree or graduated. *That* entry would have been "BA (or BS) Finance, Los Angeles College, 2001."

We leave it to you to determine whether the candidate *intended* to be misleading. Perhaps not. Perhaps he has no idea how to capture his educational experience on a résumé. While this may be true, it's also true that a quick scan of any number of résumé guidance websites will show how to list education. So perhaps we should forgive him for not knowing, and still say no for his lack of willingness to do a modicum of preparatory work for his most important professional document.

As a general rule on résumés, the candidate is supposed to capture information in a form *not* in a way that she wants to present herself, but rather in a way that *recruiters and managers want to see*. This is the résumé corollary to Horstman's Law that communication is what the listener does. The most effective and accepted way to present a university degree is: *Degree, Major, School, Location, Year Graduated*. If you see something other than that, it's time to have concerns. And if you have concerns, that's a sign that résumé needs to go in the "no" pile.

What Was the Quality Level of the Education?

This area of résumé education screening gets far less attention than it deserves. Most managers and recruiters aren't as knowledgeable—*and they easily could be*—regarding the relative quality of educational institutions worldwide. Information is readily available to a manager in the United States, for instance, that University of Melbourne, in Victoria, Australia, is regarded as the best university in Australia. They may not know that Monash University is also in Melbourne and is one of the Top 5 schools in Australia.

A degree from an IIT school in India is widely regarded as an elite degree. Entrance is extremely competitive. An NIT degree is also very well regarded, but not at the level of an IIT degree. To not know this and interview a candidate who lists one of these schools is to put oneself at a disadvantage in the screening and therefore hiring process.

Part of what makes educational quality important is the signaling effect of graduation from an institution *whose entrance requirements are known to be strict.* We mentioned the competitiveness of entrance to IIT schools in India. The U.S. equivalent might be Harvard, or Stanford, or perhaps what are known as the Ivy League schools. (There are also certainly some schools that stand out for certain industries. Wharton MBAs are famous for their financial analytical skills. Northwestern MBAs are famous for their marketing skills.)

What is important for U.S. managers is that a foreign candidate may not have any chance to go to a U.S. university whose quality is known to the manager, but the person's national/foreign university may be quite significantly more competitive than an Ivy League school for a U.S. student. *Lack of knowledge of these kinds of distinctions is a disadvantage in the hiring market.*

There are also many schools in the United States whose reputation is stellar, but that reputation is more regional than national. Rensselaer Polytechnic (RPI) is an outstanding engineering school. The same for the University of Illinois at Urbana-Champaign. Cal Tech is unknown outside of technology but is widely regarded as one of the top five engineering and science schools in the world. *It's not hard to learn these signs of quality by doing simple online searches for comparative information.*

How Did He Perform During His Education?

It's not enough that someone finished some level of education. The next question, the important question, is how well he or she performed. Isn't this the same question we have about professional performance? Not just what jobs he had, but *how well did he do them?* Not just that she spent four years at uni, but *how well did she do there?*

The first question to ask is how did he do academically? There are different ways of showing performance throughout the world. In the United States, the standard measure is grade point average (GPA). A GPA of 3.0 is good, a completely reasonable standard for above average performance (4.0 is all As. 3.5 is exceptional). The British system names its highest performance level a "First," for First Class. There is also an Upper and Lower Second, named Two-One and Two-Two, respectively. The German system is opposite of the U.S. system: 1 is the highest score, and a 4 is a low/average score. Of course, most hiring is national, and most managers know their own nation's system. But it does no good to know it and not use it as a criterion in screening.

Often, of course, we don't know the GPA from a résumé. But a new professional's résumé is likely to list various activities and honors, giving us a sense of overall performance. A fresh college graduate with no distinguishing success at school is less likely to blossom into a top performer than a graduate with signs of a high GPA, extracurricular activities, and leadership positions around campus.

A lack of high performance at university is a reason to go into the no pile.

Accuracy—What to Look For

Over half the résumés we see at Manager Tools have errors in them. Twenty-five percent have multiple errors. Accuracy matters on a résumé. Candidates know that accuracy matters, so any mistakes are a reason to be very concerned.

Candidates know that someone looking at their résumés is a go/no-go gate, and they know that accuracy is a right/wrong proposition. If we're looking for reasons to say no, *and we are,* we don't need to look any further than someone who won't work hard enough to get the details right *when getting the details right is a widely understood important factor in a process.*

Remember that a résumé is a written document. It is a form of written communication. In written communication, accuracy is considered to be quite important, and a *résumé with errors indicates a poor communicator.* Have you ever hired someone knowing— *knowing*—that she was a poor communicator? If you have, you know that you can try to overlook it, but it usually (almost always) ends poorly. That's because the single most frequent thing most of us do at work every day is communicate. If you're going to hire someone with inaccuracies on a résumé, you're hiring a poor communicator, and you're willfully planning to work with someone who is going to send you lots of emails riddled with errors. And he's going to do the same to his directs . . . and your customers.

Spelling errors are particularly egregious today. Thanks to word processing, to spell a common word incorrectly almost requires work. It is a sign of hard work, intellect, and attention to detail that people know the difference between homonyms like there and they're and their, and when to use an apostrophe on the word its.

Contrary to current common wisdom, the speed at which mobile devices allow us to do things *is not* contrary to accuracy. *That speed helps you look up every spelling, every grammar rule, every capitalization rule, in record time.* Inaccuracy is not a result of lack of tools or resources. It's a choice, a behavior, a decision. It's prioritizing speed over accuracy, *in a medium where accuracy is known to be prized and speed is an indicator of lack of preparation.*

So look for spelling errors. If you want to forgive one spelling error, fine. We would never recommend you do that, but we'll understand, and you can hire that candidate. If you're torn on what to do, put the one-error résumés in your maybe pile.

More than one error, though, is a no. Full stop. Interesting tidbit: The one area (in the United States) where résumés longer than one page stubbornly remain (we understand the reasons) is academia. Often professors' and researchers' résumés run to five and six pages. And surely in universities and research departments accuracy and attention to detail matter. But errors on academic résumés occur at a *much* higher ratio than on corporate/professional résumés.

Density—What to Look For

Density is an often-overlooked area of résumé screening. It illustrates whether or not the preponderance of the candidate's experience is relevant to your role and industry.

As a general rule, if you are not an experienced manager—in this case meaning having screened résumés many times to decide whom to interview—a low density résumé in the area of relevance to industry/role is a reason to say no.

Many managers think that "there are similarities," that "commerce is commerce," that "business is business," that "marketing is marketing," that "good developers will become good with any language." These statements are true . . . and truisms. (A truism is a statement that is true *and means nothing*.) The fact is, specific knowledge of products and particular industries matters, and taking the time to learn about them on the job is a significant drag on productivity.

Searching for relevance/density also helps us notice nonlinear career choices, lack of perseverance within a career path or an industry. Someone who moves from marketing to sales to customer service, say, in similar roles, and does so in multiple industries without significant accomplishments, and in stints of one to three years, *is likely to leave your industry, your role, your company, your team, in one to three years.* Are we hiring an employee or a contractor? How much ought we invest in career management for this person? How many conversations will we have with him or her about the future (we do that in One-on-Ones) that will be wasted?

This is not to say that a linear career path is the only way to success. That's a false dilemma. There are great candidates with unusual backgrounds who could be an outstanding fit for the role you're hiring for. Candidates with such backgrounds often make that case, sometimes even reasonably well.

But to make that case ourselves is to make the case for *reasons to hire*. We are not looking for reasons to hire, but rather for reasons to say no. The appropriate response to someone who argues that she could be an excellent hire even though her background isn't ideal is that in order to do so, we would have to be looking for reasons to hire people, which would open us up to myriad reasons for every candidate to be a good hire, because every candidate does have something to offer. If there are one million possible candidates for any one role, the only logical approach to those one million candidates is to *rule people out*, not in.

How to Decide Whom to Screen Further

This is the easy part. Armed with these criteria, *and looking for reasons to say no*, create three piles: No, Maybe, and Yes. It's completely okay to put a candidate in the Maybe pile if you have a question but his divergence from your ideal isn't significant.

It's also okay to remember that there are exceptions to all of the rules we've shared. You may just have "a sense" that a particular candidate's screening problem isn't as big a deal as it appears. It could be true. Life is never a straight line, and all of us have bumps in our roads to where we are today.

That's okay. It's your process. Put them in the maybe pile. Just don't confuse forgiving a small misstep with deciding to like the candidate. Put him or her in the maybe pile and then work through everyone in your yes pile first.

Try to apply the same criteria through your entire pile of candidates. If you're being forgiving on, say, industry with one candidate, try to remember to do that with others. Why? Because this process is subjective and far more likely to be affected by mood, desperation, and level of energy (tired screening is likely to mean "no" screening) than is obvious.

Also, start with as many résumés as you can collect. Don't let HR take your possible pile from 500 to 100 *until you know and trust your HR partners because they know you*. It doesn't take that long to say no to those extra 400 résumés. *And the more screening someone else who is not deeply engaged in the role you're hiring for does, the more danger there is that he's said yes to the wrong candidates.*

Once you've gone through the whole pool of candidates, you'll have your three piles. Throw away the "no" pile, unless you want to train your directs and HR on how you screen and why. Set aside the "maybe" pile. Phone screen the "yes" pile.

If you have too many yes's to screen them all, it's either time to do a happy dance or to recalibrate your screening process.

Résumé screening and phone screening are your most efficient tools to close in on your one hired candidate. Face-to-face interviewing is your most effective tool to choose precisely "the one."

Over time, you'll become adept at screening for the roles for which you hire. This just gives you a basic framework, upon which you can layer your particular situation . . . for something you'll do perhaps 100 times in your career. If it matters, and you're going to do it a lot, it's important to be good at it.

8

Screening Social Media

WE STRONGLY RECOMMEND YOU REVIEW the social media behaviors of potential candidates. Social media posts, activities, and profiles are indicators of the habits and character of potential candidates.

Over the years we've heard from some managers and candidates that a social media review is an "invasion of privacy." We disagree, because social media is not a private activity, but manifestly public. (We certainly don't recommend less than ethical methods to examine candidates' online activities.)

An example is helpful here. Consider the candidate who answers all of your screening questions well and seems to have the right background and experience. You bring him in for a full day of onsite interviews. This is the final step in your hiring process.

During that day of interviews, per our recommendation (explained later), you schedule a brown-bag lunch for him and three or four of your direct reports who are interviewing him that day. You're clear with him that this is *not* an interview, but nevertheless a chance to get to know him better in an informal setting. [When you're next a candidate, don't forget that, even when you're not interviewing, you're **still being evaluated**.] You're also clear that this is a chance for him to get to know you and the people he'll be working with.

During the lunch, your candidate is a surprisingly sloppy eater. He gets food on his face—which happens to us all—but then wipes it on his sleeve. He doesn't use his napkin to wipe some small spills around where he's eating. He comments that he doesn't like the food he's eating: "This isn't very good. Too salty." He interrupts others several times. When one of your team asks him about one of the companies he's worked for—after mentioning that the questioner himself worked there several years ago—the candidate says, "I thought you said this wasn't an interview. What was your experience like there?"

Our recommendation would be to not hire this candidate. Remember: The purpose of evaluating candidates is to **find reasons to say no**. Despite what are good interview answers, his behavior at lunch is rude and unprofessional. You realize: This person isn't polite.

It certainly is possible that you would disagree with this assessment. You might say, "Well, all I care about are his technical skills. We don't put much stock here in etiquette and manners and being nice to others." We would caution that you are making a mistake. There are two reasons to fire someone: either she doesn't get her job done, *or she engages in behaviors that are detrimental to team morale and communication*. The lunch behaviors are noteworthy enough to assume that these behaviors will continue. You're already assuming that his "good" behaviors/answers in his interviews are going to continue. Why not these bad ones as well? In our experience, they will.

This lunch behavior example is similar to a candidate's social media presence. When hiring, we do not confine ourselves to candidate interview answers. We look at the whole person, not just his or her narrow technical skills. *The entire candidate, with all of his or her interpersonal habits and communication foibles, will work with you.* Employees are not robots, but humans, having to work with other humans.

You might also argue that how a potential employee behaves in social media activities are (in most free countries) "free speech." This is generally true. But it is mitigated by the principle (codified by case law in most countries) that employees do not have the right to free speech in the workplace. You can't say anything you want at work and call it free speech. By the same token, employment generally follows a rule called "at will." This means you can quit for any reason, and your employer can fire you for virtually any (behavioral) reason.

Social media screening is not about looking for candidates you "agree with" politically, socially, or in hobbies or interests. This kind of screening often borders on discrimination, with which we vehemently disagree. In fact, a candidate who expresses different political views on social media than the norm or majority in your firm but does so respectfully and with intellect and compassion might well excite you. It would us.

Rather, we recommend you use social media to look for behaviors or indicators that there are professional, ethical, or communication problems that could surface at work.

Before we share some areas to look at, also remember that at Manager Tools, we make recommendations that are "timeless" and not "timely." But when it comes to social media, "timeless" is very hard to warranty.

As an example of the changing face of the technological/social media world, Manager Tools' first podcast guidance about social media was originally titled, "The MySpace Cast." That's because the cast was released in 2008, when MySpace had yet to be eclipsed by Facebook (and as of this writing, Instagram and Twitter).

As of 2019, here is our social media screening guidance:

- **LinkedIn: Does the Candidate's Profile Match His/Her Résumé?** As of this writing, LinkedIn is the most widely used professional social media site. We are astounded at the number of candidates who have glaring differences between their résumés and their public LinkedIn pages. Do they list the same companies and jobs in both their résumés and on LinkedIn? Are their jobs or companies missing on one or the other?

- **LinkedIn: Does the Candidate Have Endorsements/Recommendations and Are They for Skills You Value in This Role?** The absence of such endorsements may be an indicator. This is probably less true for a less experienced candidate. From whom are the recommendations, and how recent are they? If they're from peers (internal to their firm at the time), that weighs less than recommendations from customers or managers. If recommendations are 10 years old, it makes sense to look more closely at the candidate's résumé items from the last 10 years. Perhaps there has been a falloff in levels of performance.

- **LinkedIn: Has He/She Posted/Liked Anything That Is Objectionable to You?** Much like our previous lunch example, are there posts that cause you to question the candidate's ability to communicate professionally or work well as a teammate? If the candidate has posted to groups he or she belongs to, is the post respectful? When there are disagreements, do they do so in an agreeable way? Does he only post challenges and disagreements? Or does she like/applaud/support ideas with which she agrees?

- **Facebook/Instagram/Twitter: Are There Photos/Posts That Show This Person in a Bad Light?** The classic example of a candidate exhibiting poor judgment is a profile picture that shows the candidate drunk. Being drunk (if you're in private or not driving) isn't an issue, but publicly displaying one's drunkenness (which such a post does) is a sign of immaturity or poor judgment. We remember one candidate using his jailhouse mugshot as his profile picture. Perhaps the infraction was innocent, but publicly displaying the picture is a sign of poor judgment. This is not always so: perhaps she was arrested for a peaceful demonstration. But such online behavior ought to raise an eyebrow about someone's judgment, which will be used every day at work. As a general rule, one's judgment in one's personal life, however protected and supported by modern freedoms, is an indicator of the judgment the person will bring to your workplace.

Political expressions are protected in social media. And we show our thankfulness for those freedoms by exercising those rights. But political speech that denigrates others or opposing viewpoints is worthy of a professional consideration: Will the candidate be able to disagree in the workplace with comity and respect?

- **Has He Erased His Profiles Completely?** This may or may not be a problem, but if you don't check social media, how would you know? It worries us.
- **Software Development Candidates—StackExchange.** While the absence of a presence on StackExchange.com might not be a reason to rule a candidate out, we recommend software development managers assess candidates' presence and evaluate candidates' behaviors and contributions thereto. Are their interactions reasonable and appropriate for the medium? Similarly, in the software development world, Twitter is used to collaborate publicly. What is their profile there, and how do they behave?

All this said, use your social media review to gather information only. Add it to what you know and learn about a candidate. *We wouldn't recommend ruling out a candidate based on social media behaviors alone.* (If you understand the first principle of interviewing, it should be obvious that we *definitely* wouldn't use social media to rule someone in—although it might be a source of candidates.) On the other hand, with two final candidates, one whose social behavior doesn't fit with your culture and one whose does, make an offer to the one whose does.

9

Conducting Phone Screens

THE MANAGER TOOLS EFFECTIVE HIRING PROCESS recommends that before you bring someone into your office for a final day of interviewing, spend as much time screening the person as you can. With rare exceptions, do *more* over the phone to reduce your burden for the final full day of interviewing. Know more about the candidate through the steps listed previously before you invest the considerable resources of a full day of interviews.

Regarding resources, it's normal to be feeling the pinch of an open position and its associated undone work. It's normal to want to get someone through to the final step, hoping that he wows you and your team so that you can make him an offer. It takes fewer resources to go faster, to hire a candidate sooner.

Fight these urges. Effective managers know that it's smart to spend *more* resources on our most important decisions. Remember: The Second Principle of Effective Hiring: Set the Bar High. Our natural desire to fill an open position must be tempered by our desire to avoid the big mistake: filling it with the wrong person.

So, before we bring someone in for face-to-face interviews, we're going to conduct one or more screening interviews.

Thirty Minutes Is Enough

Thirty minutes is plenty of time to conduct a phone screen. A screen is *not* a full interview. It's a screen—a partial interview. Phone screens are generally conducted following résumé reviews and before a full day of final interviews. This is certainly not the only way to conduct an interview process, but it is the most likely to be used by most organizations. It would be considered "normal" by organizations where the hiring manager and his directs are co-located.

The purpose of a phone screen is to reduce the burden to your staff and cost to your organization of face-to-face interviews by reducing the number of candidates being considered. It is **not** to conduct a full and complete interview, but rather to provide another gate in the process.

There would be nothing surprising in conducting a series of phone screens and eliminating all candidates from contention, and therefore not conducting any final face-to-face interviews.

Remember: *the purpose of any interview is to say* **no**. More broadly: the purpose of the hiring process is to say no.

If that doesn't make sense to you initially, you're normal. Most managers think, *no, my purpose is to find my next hire. My purpose here is to fill my opening.*

But that is a mistaken purpose, leading to a dangerous confirmation bias in your interviewing. **If you are looking for reasons to hire someone, you will find those reasons.** As long as you're "looking to hire," as long as you "need" to find someone, your bias will be confirmed, and you'll see things in people that make you want to hire.

Our purpose in the hiring process is only secondarily to hire the right person. Our primary purpose is to *not have the wrong person.* If you're pausing right now, trust us: You're not hearing us wrong. We need to have a counter-intuitive approach when we interview. We need to guard against our subtle tendency to give ourselves what we want. If we start focusing on *making a hire*, as opposed to *avoiding a hiring mistake*, we start overlooking weaknesses. We find a hire . . . who comes with problems we probably should have seen.

So in the case of phone screens, more gates to have candidates go through is better. We want the candidates who want hiring to be easy to go away. We want those candidates who persist because they know that great companies set high bars to entrance.

Because we usually can't spend the time to conduct multiple full behavioral interviews on all of our possible résumé-screened candidates, but we want to start talking to them, phone screens are the perfect in-between gate before we go to face-to-face final interviews.

Again, it's been our experience that 30 minutes is plenty of time for most phone screens. *Remember, we're looking for reasons to say no to someone.* If you don't have a reason to rule someone out after 30 minutes, you probably won't find one after 45 minutes. If you still haven't found it at that point, and you figured you'd go to an hour-long phone call . . . the problem becomes that most people will struggle to get through a phone interview of an hour or longer. Phone behaviors start to deteriorate once we reach an hour's worth of time.

The bottom line with phone screens is you won't have enough time to cover enough questions to decide whether you want to make an offer to someone. That means you're going to have to balance time with results/value. Thirty minutes works best against those two opposed objectives.

And if you run long, even to 45 to 50 minutes, that's fine.

You Make the Phone Call

Many managers are surprised that we recommend that you, the manager, call the candidate. But this is simply how it's done among companies that set and maintain high recruiting standards. Recruiters and hiring managers want to send a message that "My time with you is important to me, and I care enough about it to be prepared and prompt."

Do you have to do this? No. It's not a black and white situation. There are plenty of managers who say, "I'm going to give them a time to call, and if they're not professional enough to call me at that time, that's a reason to say no." That certainly is a reasonable application of the underlying purpose of this process: to find a reason to say no.

But you making the call sends a message about your interest. And it also helps you control the interview.

Give Them a Brief Process Overview

Of course, all interviews start with brief introductions and some brief chit-chat. [You can find our guidance about the beginning of an interview in chapter seven.] In a phone screen, that might last perhaps 1 or 2 minutes. If nothing else, it's polite human interaction. You can't have the candidate answer the phone and have your first words be, "Tell me about yourself." It might be efficient, but it will affect your ability to hire (which makes it ineffective).

One of the hallmarks of effective interviewers is their forthright communication of the process candidates are going through. There is already enough stress in the process (more on this later). That stress isn't helpful. Candidates don't think that added stress beyond their own performance anxiety is professional. Further, it doesn't improve our ability to make good choices.

Finally, it's not enough that we feel our process is effective for us and our firm. *It's important to acceptance rates and future relationships that candidates feel that the process was fair and reasonable.* Candidates who are told no and believe the process they were exposed to was fair handle the rejection far better than when they feel the process was unclear, unfair, biased, insensitive, or capricious. Candidates who are told yes are more likely to accept.

So tell them what's going to happen. If you follow the Manager Tools recommended process, it might sound like this:

Before I ask you my first question, I want to explain how this process generally works. This phone screen is our first step. It will only be roughly 30 minutes long. I may only ask you 1–2–3 questions. I'm going to probe/interrupt periodically for more information. That's normal; don't worry about it. I won't have time to ask for your questions. We'll save those for an in-person interviewing day, if we take that next step. I probably won't be able to give you a yes/no answer about an invite for a personal interview during this call. I'll want to think about this and other interviews, and I may share my thoughts with others here internally. That said, you will hear from me one way or another within a week at most.

Start with "Tell Me About Yourself" (TMAY)

Then you ask the core question of the majority of phone screens: *Tell me about yourself*. We have to start somewhere . . . and in some cases, you have never spoken to this person before, and this will be the first interview question you ask. This is probably when the candidate would say the interview started.

Keep in mind that there's a difference between the actual interviews we conduct with candidates and the overall evaluation we are in the process of making. Effective managers are constantly evaluating and measuring as this process unfolds, even when they are not conducting a proper interview.

"Tell me about yourself" (TMAY) is a great first significant interview question. For the vast majority of candidates, it requires no preparation specific to your organization or role. [Of course, to an exceptionally well-prepared candidate, perhaps 10% of the answer would change depending on the opportunity for which he is interviewing.] It relies on a person's knowledge of himself, about which there can be no better expert.

Further, it's expected by most candidates, and certainly any who have done any basic preparation. They can't do an Internet search of interview preparation and not come across it. [Though they can certainly find a lot of very bad guidance on how to answer it.]

Even though it's a question that responds well to preparation, and most candidates don't do much of that very well, it still is a reassuring question to hear. It reduces somewhat the chance that fear and nerves detract from the candidate's performance. Always remember that, although our purpose is to say no, we don't want to say no to hiring a great engineer because he can't ride a unicycle. An interview is an artificial reality designed to keep people out of organizations. It's an *artificial* reality. The effective interviewer uses an interview in a professional way. There's no need to intentionally elevate stress, or play tricks, or ask the hardest questions first. Those techniques don't provide data that's useful.

Most importantly, TMAY creates numerous opportunities for probing about decisions and behaviors, which are the data that effective interviewers are looking for to compare to the requirements of the role.

Don't be surprised if an answer takes a minute. That's an insufficient answer (though you can likely blame bad Internet guidance). If that's the case, probing is required, unless the answer is disqualifying on its face.

Also don't be surprised if an answer is 10 minutes long. That may be good, though it probably isn't.

Most importantly, don't be surprised if, once you have probed repeatedly, the answer may have been 1 minute had you not interjected, but *with* your interjections you've consumed 25 minutes of the interview.

Ask One or Two Behavioral Questions, Time Permitting

If you have time following TMAY, there are no better questions than behavioral ones. This of course presupposes that you have previously prepared the interview that you will be conducting when you bring these candidates in for a final in-person day.

No Need to Share Your Decision at the Time

When finishing a phone screen, we have no data which shows that asking for questions will help you gather useful data for the decision you are making. That said, this is probably much more a function of the limited time and the assumptions that candidates make about the limited time and the "incomplete" nature of a screen versus an interview.

So end the screen by thanking the candidate, and telling her that you will be either comparing your thoughts with HR (if HR did a screen) or you will be considering how to proceed and sharing your thoughts with your team to make your decision about an in-person interview.

Phone screening is a great way to further narrow down the candidates who will go through a final full day of interviews. The planning and logistics time and expense justify adding an additional screening filter between résumés and final interviews. The process to do it is simple.

10

Having Human Resources Conduct Phone Screens

THERE ARE MANY PLACES WHERE the process/policy is that HR conducts phone screens in the place of managers. This is, in principle, a good idea, because it's yet another gate, another screen, another set of eyes looking for reasons to say no. And in the case of HR, versus you and your directs and perhaps one or two peers, they're going to have a different perspective. That's good.

But . . . there's a huge misunderstanding that occurs when HR conducts phone screens as policy. What happens is many managers think that HR conducting "A" phone screen means that HR is therefore conducting "the only" phone screen. That HR "owns" the phone screen process. In most cases, we'd guess, managers assume that HR is doing some special, different, HR-informed, previously trained phone screen of which the manager is incapable, and for which the manager is unauthorized.

This is a laughably wrong conclusion in 90% of situations. Don't assume that HR is doing *the* phone screen (as if there is such a thing). Don't assume that HR is therefore doing the *only* phone screen. Don't assume that HR is the phone screener of record for your firm.

BTW: What is HR *doing* in a phone screen? It depends on the experience of your HR professional. Almost every HR phone screen includes some obligatory information about the company (meaning the HR person is talking—briefing the candidate, versus evaluating the person). There are probably some assertions regarding equal opportunity and nondiscrimination. There are probably some comments about company values and principles designed to differentiate your company from the competition and marketplace.

But as you might imagine, HR listens differently to most candidate answers. Except in the case of an experienced HR professional with whom the hiring manager has a solid relationship (about which more below), the typical HR phone screen is about screening for cultural and organizational fit. *Is this person right **for our company**? Does this person have the values we look for?* And in most cases, HR is evaluating communication skills during the phone screen and "tell me about yourself" question (if they ask it).

What does this all tell us we should do? Let's assume the most likely situation: a moderately experienced HR representative, with whom you have a good but not extensive relationship, and who doesn't have the background in your area to be evaluating job skills.

Here we have three choices. The most common situation is you let HR conduct "the" phone screen, and you accept their input to narrow your field of candidates (assuming they do). You *don't* conduct your own phone screen and go right to taking whomever they "passed" to a final set of face-to-face interviews on site.

This is the wrong choice.

The combination of a lack of a strong relationship and the lack of your HR partner's knowledge of your work means that solely relying on the HR screening process is misguided. The likelihood that HR is calibrated to what you're looking for is **very small**, so their evaluation of candidates is not related to your role and biases about skills, abilities, traits, and characteristics. Their opinions will not be predictive of a candidate's success.

That leaves us two options: (a) phone screen everyone that HR does or (b) phone screen only those candidates that your HR partner passes on to you. If you feel you can do it politically (meaning HR won't act as if it truly is *only* HR's role to phone screen and try to "forbid" you), Manager Tools recommends you phone screen everyone that HR did.

If you need verbiage for HR, it would sound like this: *I really appreciate the phone screen, and I'm sure you're right about everyone. And I'm a relatively inexperienced interviewer, so me getting a sense of more candidates would be **very** helpful to me. Also, your criteria are of course different from mine, and while I'm likely to agree with you, us both interviewing will give us a chance to calibrate on this role and my preferences. Finally, I may be able to screen further, so there's less burden on my team when a smaller group comes in for final interviews.*

If you're not comfortable with the potential politics or tension there, we recommend you choose to conduct an additional phone screen on those candidates that HR recommends you continue to interview. The downside of this technique is that if you're working with an HR partner that you don't have a well-established relationship with, you won't have the opportunity to calibrate your evaluation with his . . . and you may end up stuck with a perpetually low-value relationship.

You could say this in that situation: *Thanks for doing the screening. Just so I can get to know the candidates that you've recommended, I'm also going to do phone screens on each of them. That will help me share some information with my team—who will be interviewing the candidates as well—before they have to sit down with them for a more in-depth interview.*

As an aside, you may end up hiring someone that HR screened and passed and surmise from that that you *are* calibrated. But we can't really know that without knowing whether or not there were candidates whom they said *no* to who might have been a fit as well.

If you *do* have an experienced HR partner, she knows your role and has screened or even interviewed for it before, and you have developed a strong relationship with her over time, first: Well Done! HR partners like these are some of your most important colleagues. Let them do your phone screens.

And of course, there's a possibility that you don't have an HR organization, or even if you do, this is not something they are involved in. That's common and not problematic. Conduct phone screens on every candidate who made it through your résumé and application culling. Or if you have a great relationship with a stellar HR person, and he's presently not involved in your screening and hiring process, why not include him? If he knows your role and knows your needs and team, he can often either add additional perspective or some labor sharing, or both.

SECTION
4

Conducting Interviews

11

Video and Telephone Interviews

THERE ARE SOME CASES WHEN candidates are distant from you, and your firm will not pay for face-to-face interviews. While this carries a great deal more risk, Manager Tools recognizes that what's ideal and what's possible are often far apart. We give guidance on what's possible.

You *can* substitute a series of phone/video interviews for the full day of face-to-face interviews described in the next chapters. But you increase your risk of a bad hire.

In that case, conduct several *video* interviews following the full-day format described in upcoming chapters. Have several of your directs interview the candidate for an hour or longer. Then you conduct (yes, even after your original phone screen) a one-to-two hour video interview.

Video is almost always preferable to a phone interview. It is well established that a great deal of the information we gather communicating with others involves facial expressions and body language (beyond just the words they say and how they say them, which is all a phone screen gives us).

The one case when a series of phone screens alone may be tolerable is when limited bandwidth creates frequently dropped calls and an inability to develop the feeling that you're having a normal face-to-face conversation. We still recommend that you consider the logistics of having the candidate or your interviewers go somewhere where bandwidth is not an issue.

12

Effective Final Interview Process

YOU'VE AVOIDED HIRING INITIALLY. You've set the bar high. You've decided to look for reasons to say no. You've established your hiring criteria. You've created questions based on those criteria. You've screened résumés, perhaps in conjunction with your HR business partner. You've screened candidates' social media. You've conducted phone screens based on our guidance. Now it's time to conduct a full day of onsite interviews with those candidates who remain.

When communicating with your candidate and arranging logistics, tell him exactly what the interviewing day is going to be. *There is no value in surprising candidates or making them guess about what's going to happen.*

Our interviewing and hiring data show that maintaining some kind of secrecy about your process does not increase your chances of finding true positives or true negatives. It does, however, decrease your chances of offers being accepted. Candidates often tell us that a company not communicating its process is perceived to be hiding that they have no process. Further, candidates tell us that companies who tell them their process in advance and then follow that process closely are perceived to be more professional, more fair, *and more likely to have determined accurately who will be a fit for them and who won't.*

Sharing your final interview process beforehand will increase the chances that you will hire whom you offer, and those whom you decline will consider your declination fair and reasonable, and be more accepting of it.

Here's an example schedule for a final onsite interview day:

9:00	Hiring Manager Logistics Overview
9:30	Interview with Lauren Woods
10:45	Bathroom Break
10:50	Interview with Eldon Lukas
12:00	Interview with Wendy McGuire
1:00	Team Lunch, Conference Room
2:15	Interview with Dan Schaffer
3:15	Interview with Anandha Dreyer
4:15	Bathroom Break
4:20	Final Interview, Trevor West

You Start—(30) Minutes—No Interview—Brief Logistics

Before your candidate starts formally interviewing with you on the final day, take time to brief her in detail on exactly what's going to happen. There are several reasons for this.

First, you want to give her a chance to calm down a bit. Candidates are nervous at the start of the interviewing day. Despite the way many managers talk about seeing how people perform under stress, *there's no evidence that increasing interviewing stress levels improves the likelihood of an effective hiring decision.* Further, we have seen repeatedly that simple attempts to *reduce* interviewing stress increases the likelihood of true positives and true negatives.

The fact is, normal levels of interviewing stress are enough. In our work, we've seen that interviewing stress is different enough from work stress that increasing it isn't a useful tool in making good assessments.

Second, you want to walk candidates through their interviewing day. You will have already communicated their schedule. Frequently, the schedule will have changed. This first meeting gives you the chance to give them the final version of their interview schedule.

We recommend you start with a brief welcome. Explain to the candidate that you want them to know what's going to happen, and when. Tell them that this isn't an interview, but what amounts to an in-briefing. [This is no reason to not be *evaluating* the candidate, much as you will do if they come to work for you.]

Give them the schedule, with the names of everyone they're interviewing with on it, and the times and locations of those interviews. If you're having them go from office to office, or cubicle to cubicle, give them a simple map to show them where everything is.

Make sure you give them your team's phone numbers to text or call if they have a problem. You will have given everyone on your team a copy of the schedule. The best way to do this is by email. Ideally, you will have briefed your team at your most recent weekly staff meeting. Tell them all then that everyone is responsible for the candidate having a good experience. They'll be on alert for the candidate getting lost or someone being late to an interview.

Tell the candidate, that as the schedule shows, he'll be having a non-interview lunch with a small group. He'll also finish the interview day with you, assuming all goes well. Finally, answer any questions he has and escort him to the first interview.

You'll discover with this kind of full interviewing day that it's very difficult to bring in multiple candidates on the same day. We understand the efficiency of bringing multiple candidates in on the same day; travel schedules, and unmovable meetings make scheduling days like this more difficult.

But if you bring in multiple candidates on the same day, there are two detractors to making good hiring decisions. First, logistics get much harder. A crisis or a significant change in someone's schedule means one or both candidates will not be fully evaluated. They'll also feel like they didn't have the best chance to make their best impression.

Second, and more importantly, *candidates who are interviewed on the same day are inevitably compared to one another*. Most managers are surprised to hear this isn't effective, but it isn't.

Believe it or not, hiring is not about comparing candidates and picking the best one. We illustrate this at our Effective Hiring Manager Conference with a scenario.

Consider three candidates. At the end of the process, there's a ranking in many folks' minds: Candidate A is best, B next, and C last. The normal assumption is that candidate A is your choice.

But that's not right. A may be the best of the three, **but candidate A may still not meet your criteria for hiring**. She may be best, but that only means the best of three "no's."

There is a greater likelihood of a "comparing candidates" mindset among your team when you bring candidates in on the same day.

The question every interviewer should be asking is "Is this candidate right for the job?" Full stop. Ranking candidates against one another is not the mindset to have. Rather, the comparison should be between each candidate and the requirements of the role.

If you're going to consider ranking candidates, *do this only with the candidates whom your process deems meet the requirements of the job*. Only when more than one candidate gets unanimous approval (more on this later) in the Interview Results Capture Meeting should there be a discussion about which to hire.

What often happens with the comparative mindset is that interviewers get fixated on their "best" candidate. This is often made more difficult when different interviewers rank the candidates differently.

Further, if there are two or more candidates who meet your standards, your first choice may not accept your offer. That's a problem we solve with the timing of offer deadlines and the communications we have with candidates once we start making offers, which we'll discuss later.

It is easier and smarter to bring one candidate in on any day, and tell your interviewers *not* to compare him or her to any other candidate, but to the standard each has to meet to receive an offer. Tell them that if you're stuck with an embarrassment of riches at the end, you'll deal with that at that time.

(All) of Your Directs Interview

This full or nearly full day of interviews is your last chance to get as complete a sense of the candidate as you can. It makes no sense to interview someone for only one or two or even three hours if you can learn more in six or seven hours, since you might be committing to spending years with the person.

Not spending this time to make the right decision puts efficiency over effectiveness. When we hire at our firm, we sometimes conduct 20 to 30 hours of interviews, and sometimes more. This supports the principle that the only thing worse than that open position is filling it with the wrong hire.

We say "all" because it depends on the number of directs you have. Six or seven interviews is usually possible if a candidate is there for the full day, you have a group lunch, and you take 90 minutes to two hours to interview the person at the end of the day. If you have five directs, we recommend all of them interview, assuming they are ready to do so. But if you have 10 directs, not all can interview.

A member of your team who isn't experienced in interviewing may not be ready to interview. However, to get experience, she can start by sitting in on another interview. If she does this, she should sit out of the sight of the candidate. (Behind the candidate usually works.) Have the direct conducting the interview explain that the other team member is *not* part of the interview. This avoids any danger—and it is a danger—of the candidate feeling that he is in a panel interview (which we'll cover later).

Once your inexperienced team member has done that one or two times, she can be on a candidate's schedule. You could choose to not have her input considered from her first actual interview when you ask for recommendations during the Interview Results Capture Meeting.

Don't be too aggressive in scheduling the interview day. If the candidate has back to back to back to back interviews with no breaks, he'll feel at a disadvantage. Your team members must know that they have to finish their interviews on time and allow time for the candidate to be on time to the next interview. Usually, you'll want the team members to escort the candidate to the next interview when they have finished.

If you only have three directs, that leads to a shorter day. That's fine. If you want, ask an experienced peer of yours to conduct an interview. Only do so, though, if he or she agrees to follow your guidance on the interview. You will have already told the candidate that you have a standard way of interviewing. If your peer doesn't want to follow it, that's his call, probably, but then don't have him interview. We've seen peers do things their own way and share their disagreement with the process with the candidate. That's not a helpful message to your potential hires.

Better/More Experienced Performers Get 75 or More Minutes

Have your more experienced interviewers interview in the morning. Give them more time—even 90 minutes if you think they can use more time to make a better decision. Schedule them in the morning to decrease the chances that changes in the day's events would cause their interviews to be changed, shortened, or even cancelled.

Less Experienced Interviewers Get 60 Minutes

Less experienced interviewers are less likely to probe well and to learn as much as a more experienced interviewer. Generally, schedule them after the more experienced members of your team.

90 Minutes for Lunch

This is not a hard-and-fast rule. (In our example schedule, the lunch is brown bag in the conference room, and this only requires 75 minutes.) Ninety minutes is necessary if you choose to have a group go offsite. Offsite isn't better, but sometimes it's your best option.

The reason we recommend 90 minutes is because if you do have to go offsite, there is travel time to consider. *You don't want the uncertainties of time to and from, late arrivals, and slow service to create problems with your afternoon interview schedule.*

Lunch is informal, not an interview with an interview format. Of course, you are still evaluating the candidate. Ask how the day is going. Encourage your team to keep it conversational, though certainly questions are part of any normal conversation.

Act as a facilitator of the discussion at lunch while keeping an eye on time and, if you're offsite, pay the bill paid quickly so you won't be delayed. Encourage team members to include the candidate in the conversation. It would be normal in a team lunch for some members of your team to make comments and exchange ideas with *each other* rather than the candidate having to talk 50% of the time. And your candidate needs time to eat!

You Interview Last for 90–120 Minutes

Your interview is last of the day, usually. You'll want more time, because you will be taking responsibility for the candidate if he or she accepts an offer.

End with the Interview Results Capture Meeting. We'll discuss this in Chapter 20.

13

Physical Interview Setup

As a general rule, we don't recommend putting a candidate in one conference room for the day of interviews. This often seems an efficient way of handling things, but candidates *don't like it*. They feel sequestered. They comment afterward that they didn't get a good feeling for the workplace. You won't get better interviews, but you may get fewer offer acceptances.

If you must do this due to security concerns, that's understandable. Tell the candidate why you're doing it in advance. And make sure your interviewers know that this means they will have to work very hard to be promptly in some other place than their office/cubicles. There is an epidemic of lateness to meetings everywhere we go: Don't let the candidate's interviews just be "another meeting I can be late to" for your team.

A conference room is often chosen in open plan offices. But having an open plan office usually isn't a good enough reason for the (bad) solution of using a conference room. You can conduct a great interview sitting in your open plan desk space. Others will hear parts of the interview, yes. But that's what the candidate will experience if she comes to work for you. Interestingly, the latest version of conference rooms, often called "huddle rooms," are even worse if the candidate stays there all day. Usually the rooms are unscheduled, so they're available, but they're just too small for a candidate to stay in all day. They can be a little claustrophobic.

If your open plan office is too crowded (it usually isn't, but sometimes is), the conference room may be inevitable. If so, give the candidate a tour, explain the office set up, and encourage her to say hello to team members who are not interviewing.

Discourage your interviewers from chatting too much about the candidate during the rest of their day. An early interview that goes poorly and then is communicated to others inhibits later interviewers from giving the candidate a full and fair interview.

Each interview stands on its own. Each interviewer is usually going to have somewhat equal input into your hiring decision. An interviewer who doesn't give her all diminishes the process, and may be surprised by how other interviewers report at the end of the day.

For team members who have their own offices, have them conduct their interviews there. If there is no space other than to conduct the interview across the desk, that's acceptable but not ideal.

An across-the-desk interview is off-putting to candidates. A desk puts the interviewer in even more of a superior role than is required. Candidates describe cross-desk interviews as being less friendly and less conversational.

If you can move from behind your desk, do so. A couch for the candidate and an armchair for you, at 90 degrees, is a great choice. You may have to use a clipboard to hold your notes, but that's fine.

Despite what most professionals believe, a totally effective interview can be conducted in most cubicles. Sometimes that means across the "tongue" of your cube's desk (that's what it's called) where you would have a colleague sit across from you in a two-person meeting. Or you can use two chairs in your cubicle, close together, again using a clipboard for your note taking.

Perhaps the biggest problem with interviewing in your cubicle, office, or even in your area in an open plan office *is the distractions for the interviewer*. If there is a computer screen, open laptop, a tablet or iPad, or even your phone between you and your candidate, *you will get distracted.*

We can't tell you the number of times a manager has said to us, "Oh, I'm not using that. I'm going to ignore it." We then say, "That's fine, if you're not going to look at it, just quit your mail client software." And the response is nearly always, "But if I'm not going to look at it, why would I need to shut down mail?" We have stopped telling them that if they're not going to look at it, why would shutting their mail client down matter?

Most of these very same managers are aghast when we show them videotape of an interview *with their eyes averting to the screen nearly every minute.*

Some of this is just all the alerts that managers get, for Slack, and mail, and instant messaging. But if you're a long-time listener to Manager Tools, you know that those alerts need to be turned off. Handling email throughout your day, rather than scheduling time to focus on it, is a huge productivity drain.

One final note on physical setup and distractions: It's not just that you're distracted. *The visible screen between you and your candidate sends a message that those distractions are available to you.* Candidates don't like it. Maybe you're one of the rare managers who truly can ignore the distractions—you're not, but anyway—you're still hurting your organization's chances of getting a great candidate because he feels like you weren't willing to give your very best to him for even 60 to 90 minutes.

Open or shared public spaces in an office are also quite serviceable for an interview. The key here is not to choose a public space where someone not involved in the interview would sit next to you—in earshot—for more than a few minutes. If that happens, politely mention that you're conducting an interview, and the person will move away.

14

No Panel Interviews

PANEL INTERVIEWS—THREE, FOUR, OR FIVE interviewers all interviewing one candidate simultaneously—are a fairly common technique. You'll note that we don't have one in our recommended final interview schedule.

Do not use panel interviews, ever. They are the most common form of interviewing stupidity of which we are aware.

Since they are so common, you may be faced with deciding whether or not to use them. Here's why you should not use panel interviews.

Reason Why Not #1: The Right Way

The way to conduct all interviews is one interviewer interviewing one candidate. The reason for this is the primary engine of great interviewers: *The result of each interview is a hiring decision.* Either the interviewer decides to recommend hiring or not. Your recommendation to the hiring manager is the equivalent of "I would hire this person." Period.

If you are interviewing a candidate, *you are not contributing to someone else's decision on the hiring. You are deciding yourself to hire or not hire.* The burden of this recommendation responsibility is enormous. Good hiring builds organizations; bad hiring destroys organizations.

The vast majority of corporate interviews are ineffective and inefficient, because the interviewer lacks the responsibility to make a decision and the training/knowledge to conduct an effective interview.

Many managers or interviewers would say at this point: "Well, okay, but that's just not the way it works in my firm. Several of us interview a candidate, and we tell our boss (or whoever the hiring manager is) what we think, and she makes the decision."

This is a common mistake of hiring manager guidance to other interviewers: not clearly setting the responsibility of a hiring decision with each interviewer. But that doesn't mean you as an interviewer can't take the effective approach and *interview as if you had to hire this person yourself, in the next hour.* Very few managers would say, Well, if that's my responsibility, *I want to [as would happen in a panel interview] cede 50–60–70 percent of the data I'm going to gather to a bunch of other people's questions . . . especially others whom I'm pretty sure don't know what they're doing and won't feel the same sense of responsibility that I do.*

If you have to make the hiring decision—and don't kid yourself, *you do*—you ought not be sharing the limited time of an interview with others who don't care as much as you do.

Any halfway decent interviewer doesn't want to have to listen to a bunch of dumb questions or allow a candidate to ramble incessantly because someone else on the panel isn't smart enough to know that the clock is your enemy. And you're not going to get any better as an interviewer listening to worse questions than you yourself could ask. You might as well play tennis with someone not as good as you in the hopes of improving your game.

Reason Why Not #2: Loss of Multiple Effective Perspectives

Often panel interviews are touted as allowing more "perspective" on a candidate. One person asks a question, but many people listen to the answer and then share their perspectives. In fact, panel interviews do just the opposite: *they decrease perspective.*

First, if you and I are interviewing together, *I* have to make a decision based on *your* questions. Yes, you may ask a question that I wouldn't . . . but the vast majority of questions asked in interviews today are horrible. What good is saving time (one of the reasons for panel interviews) only to listen to time-wasting questions?

There's also the chance that we don't understand the rationale for another's question. How do we evaluate the answer? Imagine that someone asked a question you wouldn't have asked, you actually liked the answer, and the questioner tells you later that that answer was the reason he eliminated the candidate.

What if a panelist asks a good question, and there are so many bad probes and interjections you never get to ask the probes you need to find out whether the candidate has or does not have what you need to say yes or no?

More perspectives based on bad questions and surface responses create more ineffective, shallow perspectives. Panel interviews create the wrong kind of perspectives.

Reason Why Not #3: Negative Correlation to Effectiveness

We could have easily made this guidance much shorter by simply stating the data/facts:

- **Panel interviews do not increase the number of true positive hires.** True positives are hires that are made and turn out to be effective. Panel interviews do not help us identify good candidates.
- **Panel interviews do increase the number of false positive hires.** Panel interviews tend to create more situations where candidates are hired who should not have been. The general conclusion I draw from this is that panels diminish the likelihood of the in-depth knowledge that helps panelists decide to stand their ground on why someone isn't a good fit.

Reason Why Not #4: Candidates *Hate* Them

Hate is not too strong a word. Panel interviews are more stressful for candidates, taking them from eustress to distress. Candidates describe them as overbearing, unpredictable, and unfair. Job candidates say they understand they have to be interviewed, but an interview in most candidates' minds is one on one. More interviewers stacks the deck against them. To do that, in the service of efficiency for the hiring company, feels like piling on.

Here's the gruesome bottom line: Greater percentages of candidates who are made offers from companies who use panel interviews turn those offers down, all things being equal.

Why be more efficient at the expense of effectiveness?

Don't do panel interviews. They don't work, and candidates hate them. Whenever you're doing something really important, making any choice that substitutes efficiency for effectiveness is a bad idea.

But what if you're told you "have to"? Panel interviews are widespread despite their lack of effectiveness.

There are a number of factors to consider in this situation. Consider your political capital, whether HR has a great deal of control, and your level of trust in your HR Business Partner (HRBP), among others. At a high level, make sure that you understand the difference between a fellow manager saying, "That's how it's done here" and "Panel interviews are mandatory."

Far too many managers give up control of their hiring process because they mistake "that's how it's done" with "mandatory." **Many managers have a lot more leeway to do things their own way when they hear, "That's how it's done."** It's often the case that "That's how it's done" is another way of saying, "Lots of managers here don't have their own process for hiring, and don't want to push back on panel interviews."

We would even argue that "Panel interviews are mandatory" isn't a requirement to conduct a panel. Again, it depends on who's saying it, what the culture is, and how much power HR has.

This all boils down to whether you believe you *must* conduct a panel interview or not.

If you don't have to, don't. We hope the case we made earlier is sufficient motivation. Schedule your interviews as we suggested in Chapter 12.

If you must, support it minimally. Arrange your interviewing day well in advance, and include one spot for the panel. Notify HR of what the time slot is. Let them arrange everything around what you're doing. (It disappoints us when HR says hiring managers are in charge of their hiring, and then insists that the panel interview take precedence over all other activities, and then moves the panel time slot one or two times, and then takes two or three—or even five—days to "gather" panel data.)

You'll have to change the guidance you give slightly in your in-briefing, informing candidates that they will have a panel interview which won't follow the general approach you'll have laid out for them. Do not in any way, however, disparage the panel interview. There's a difference between not using its conclusions and airing organizational dirty laundry in front of candidates.

We generally recommend against having any of your direct reports participate on the panel. It's a waste of time, usually, because the questions that are asked won't be core to the skills you've determined are most relevant for your hire. But it may be politically useful to not push back when HR requests one of your directs to be on the panel.

If you do allow one of your directs to serve on the panel, *also schedule them to conduct their own separate interviews using your pre-planned questions.* Tell them to ask the minimum number of questions they can during the panel and to avoid sharing strong opinions during any panel discussions. It's unlikely that the panel results will happen the day of the interview, so it won't matter. You'll have made your decision (and communicated it, I hope) before "the panel's opinion" is communicated.

If for some reason HR allows you to set up the panel, put some of your directs on it who aren't ready to interview. Give them some of the questions your actual interviewers will use. Tell them this is an opportunity to practice asking questions, taking notes, probing for behaviors, and making hiring decisions, without the weight of the actual responsibility.

Reason Why Not #5: They're Not Safer

Panel interviews are sometimes argued for as a "safer" alternative than a series of 1-to-1 interviews. Somehow it's unsafe for someone to interview someone else alone. Somehow we all need a nanny, a minder. There's the fear that the interviewee will be able to make a claim that the interviewer engaged in some sort of nefarious, illicit, unprofessional, or illegal behavior.

By this logic, any company who forbade by policy any 1-to-1 interviewing would similarly ban all two-person meetings.

To be clear, this issue isn't legal: There are no codified prohibitions against 1-to-1 interviews. (And rest assured it happens all the time at the executive level.) What any such policy does is address the risk of some sort of accusation.

If you want to assess the risk of 1-to-1 interviews, scour the legal world for cases involving claims made in 1-to-1 interviews. They're virtually nonexistent. There are so many other things we're doing differently than the average manager that the "safety" benefit of panel interviews doesn't exist:

- Our job description suggests high standards.
- We will have reviewed résumés to significantly narrow down the applicant pool.
- We will have phone screened to further narrow the pool.

- At this point the risk of a problem is miniscule, but we go still further:
  - Every interviewer will be asking the same questions. Verbatim.
  - Every interviewer will have been trained, which will include interview risk factors.
  - Every interviewer will be required to support his or her hiring recommendations *only with behaviors in the interview.*

1-to-1 interviews aren't really risky, but even if you accept that they might be, all these steps will indemnify you. And if you're still worried, panels aren't the answer anyway.

15

How to Conduct Technical Interviews

IF YOU'RE HIRING SOMEONE WHOSE job requires technical skills, assess those skills as directly as you can. *Test them*. As mentioned in the beginning of Chapter 5, testing technical skills for a technical job *is in fact a behavioral interview, focusing on technical behaviors*.

Do the testing in a separate interview. Don't make the classic mistake of having every technical person spend 20 to 40% of his or her interview time making some insufficient attempt to verify a candidate's technical *skills*. At the end of that interview, they won't know enough about the candidate's technical skills and they won't know enough about other behaviors addressed in the behavioral interviews.

So one of your interviews on the final interview day addresses nothing but technical skills. The outcome of this interview is a hire/not hire recommendation based on the technical skills assessed.

Based on the types of problems you assign, do you need to provide 5 minutes for this problem, 15 for that to fill up 60 or 90 minutes?

Some examples of problems and questions: If you're hiring someone who needs to be an expert in MS Excel, give a test to see whether he can create a pivot table. Give him a dataset—rows and columns of data in Excel—on a laptop, and give him 30 minutes to create it. (If you think this is trivial, you only have to assign it one time to have people fail, all of whom described themselves as MS Office experts.)

If you're hiring a mechanical engineer, ask her to work out a simple heat transfer problem. You have an energy source, emitting radiation of X kilojoules, and a black body. With these equations and the data shown, determine the rate of absorption of the black body.

If you're hiring a software developer, give him a recursive word break problem. Or some code in a language that your firm uses (and remaining candidates likely know) with a bug in it, and ask him to debug it. Or give her a function to solve that would legitimately be part of your internal applications, and ask her to use pseudo-code to create the function.

If you're hiring a structural engineer, give him a series of problems one of which might be, "Here's a diagram of some loads on a beam. What's the deflection mid-span, and what's the reaction at the connection point?"

If the candidates are going to have to write (versus type) their answers, have them do so at a white board. If the problem requires computer entry, connect a laptop to a large monitor. When we conduct a "normal" behavioral interview, we are "observing" behaviors by listening to their answers. In a technical interview, you get to observe the skills in real time.

Don't be afraid to probe people's efforts as they work through a problem. You interject here just as you would in other behavioral interviews. For instance, "Sorry to interrupt here, why that choice? Why not wait to do that calculation later?" or "Excuse me, help me understand that. What if you didn't have access to that array?"

If you want more guidance on hiring software developers, I highly recommend one of the best professional books I've ever read: *Smart and Gets Things Done* by Stack Exchange Co-Founder Joel Spolsky.

16

Each Interviewer Uses the Same Set of Questions

AT THIS POINT, WE'VE SUGGESTED several steps in hiring that either aren't trained or are very different from what you've learned or know. (This is particularly true of this chapter.) We encourage you, once you've laid out your preparation for your next hire, to bring your direct reports together and walk them through what you've done, how this process is different, and how their roles will be, in some, cases quite different than they have perhaps grown accustomed to.

We discussed earlier that before you start this process, you're going to develop a list of behavioral interview questions. These questions are based on the job you envision your new direct doing.

These questions form the core of each and every interviewer's evaluation of the candidate.

This is at the heart of effective interviewing: Each candidate is being compared to one job. The job is the same, so each candidate is compared to the same job against the same basic criteria. This not only produces more effective results (more true positives and true negatives, and fewer false positives and false negatives), but it is also seen as more fair by candidates.

What is typical in interviewing today looks to those of us who have studied and measured interviews and outcomes as utter chaos. The idea that one interviewer (let alone all of them) could give three fundamentally different interviews to three different candidates is ludicrous. Easier, yes. Requires less preparation, yes. But measurable? No. Fair? Absolutely not. Repeatable? No way.

The ancient Buddhist parable of the three blind men touching an elephant comes to mind. Three blind men come upon an elephant and endeavor to determine what they have found. One touches the trunk and thinks he's found a fat snake. One touches a leg and describes a tree. And one touches the tail and thinks he's found a vine. And they're all wrong. The *Rigveda* says, *Reality is one, but wise men speak of it variously.*

Do not allow your team members to come up with their own idiosyncratic set of questions. Do not allow some "experienced" direct to "go with his gut." Don't allow interviewers to not prepare. [Have you ever had an interviewer ask you for your résumé at the start of an interview?] If one of your team members wants to proceed this way, don't allow that person to interview.

Very few professionals receive any interviewing training to speak of. Those who do describe a largely HR-centric briefing about how to avoid lawsuits due to discrimination. This is necessary, but hardly sufficient.

Here's an example of most professionals' profound lack of knowledge of effective and legal interviewing. You probably yourself believe (and have been taught) that there are "illegal" questions one must avoid when interviewing. In fact, this is **not true** in most locations. In the United States right now, there are only a few municipalities where asking a particular question is in itself unlawful.

The questions themselves are not illegal: Using the answers to those questions to discriminate in the hiring process is what is illegal.

We're certainly not recommending you ask a female candidate whether she is planning on having children in the next five years. It's a stupid and selfish question. It's indicative of someone who would discriminate on the basis of the answer. We want you to avoid any sort of discrimination other than the natural process of selecting the best candidate, irrespective of gender or race or ethnicity or any other orientation other than ability to do the work exceptionally well. In fact, there are enough places where this kind of scurrilous discrimination is practiced that an ethical, prepared, and unbiased interviewer increases the chances of hiring those who are often discriminated against.

But don't confuse discrimination in hiring with illegal questions. If your firm does do more in-depth, substantive interview training like we do at our Effective Hiring Manager Conferences, count yourself lucky. It's rare.

The Importance of Asking the Same Questions

What this all means is simple: *Every interviewer must ask roughly the same basic set of questions of each candidate.* Again, each interviewer is comparing each candidate against the criteria for one job. We're not comparing candidates yet—that *only* happens when more than one candidate gets over the high bar you've set for the single job you're trying to fill. *Effective interviewing is not about comparing candidates to one another—it's about comparing each candidate to the role.*

If you've done your preparatory work, you already have those questions. An example of an administrative assistant interview that we have used at Manager Tools is included for you in the Appendix, created using our proprietary Interview Creation Tool available to licensees of our work.

Every interviewer receives the same predetermined list of questions. The questions are one per page, in order of importance. You'll notice that every page has the question at the top, and the vast majority of the page is blank for note taking (more on that later).

You may be thinking, Wait! Every interviewer is going to ask each candidate the same questions? Won't the candidate get better throughout the day? Won't every candidate sound great by the last interview? Won't they all start to get frustrated with the same questions over and over? Won't they say, "Well, I already answered that question?"

The answers to those questions are no, no, no, and only the weak candidates. Keep in mind that you've chosen the questions that get at the most important behaviors of the job. Why wouldn't you want multiple interviewers to hear each candidate's answers to them?

Candidates *do not* get better throughout their day, *unless they are very well prepared and can hone an already very good answer through repetition*. We have tested this repeatedly.

Candidates describe themselves as getting better throughout the day, but interviewers do not describe seeing that in candidates. What's more, in many cases, later in the day interviewers describe candidates as becoming overconfident and not working as hard in their interviews.

The fact is, targeted, well-prepared questions make interviews *much harder* **for less prepared candidates**. This is what we want—to raise the bar. [While we are sad if we miss a good candidate every once in a while, we will tolerate that less than ideal outcome to avoid *at all costs* someone who isn't right for us getting through some easier, less targeted questions.]

In general, candidates are not well prepared for interviews. You've probably experienced this if you've interviewed a few times. Candidates are poorly served by the vast majority of Internet guidance.

Some examples of current guidance that are nonsense:

"Preparation should be about the company." This is ludicrous. The interview will be almost exclusively about the candidate's background and skills. Most candidates do not prepare enough by knowing what they've done, how well they've done it, and the behaviors they can bring to the job.

"Interview the interviewer." Even more ludicrous. If you're someone who is impressed by a candidate asking you questions, you're making decisions based on your gut. You're vastly increasing the chances of a Hell on Earth outcome. How can we know whether a candidate has the right skills for our job without probing past performance for behaviors?

"Learn to be a storyteller in interviews." Slightly less ludicrous, but still dumb. Most business conversations are not about storytelling, but about accuracy, and structure, and knowledge of facts. Too many candidates think that they can be truthfully persuasive, meaning they start by trying to persuade, and do their best to be truthful. When you think about it, what you want is for candidates to be persuasively truthful. That is, start with the truth about themselves, and then do their best to show those truths in the best possible light.

"Answer a question with a question." Really? How well does that work in relationships? How well does that work with your boss where you work now? How would you feel if your colleagues always did that with you? Idiotic.

By the way, all of these nostrums are peddled by folks who either (a) don't know any better or (b) know what it takes to succeed in interviewing (hard preparatory work and practice), but know most candidates want simple answers because they're unwilling to do the work.

Preparation Makes for a Productive Interview

Your best candidates—those with both the right background and the preparation to demonstrate it verbally in an interview—*shine* in prepared behavioral interviews. They know that less prepared candidates don't have detailed answers about their past.

Further, the best candidates *don't like* unstructured interviews. They see interviewers who don't have prepared and targeted questions as being unprepared. They report feeling like the hiring process boils down to "whomever they 'liked' best," rather than who had the best background and fit.

This is not to say that cultural and personality fit are not crucially important in your hiring process. *They are*. It takes both cultural fit as well as behavioral job fit for your best hires. The problem with unstructured, "gut" or idiosyncratic interviews is that while they may give you a "feeling" for the candidate, *you won't learn enough about his skills and abilities to go with your estimation of his personality*.

On the other hand, *you will be able to gain plenty of cultural/personality fit information in a structured behavioral interview*. The prepared nature of the questions means you won't be committing the most frequently committed sin of novice interviewers: anxiously thinking about what your next question will be when you should be listening to the answer to the question you already asked. *Candidates notice when you're not totally focused on their answers*.

This kind of interview also causes managers to ask, "But how will we get different perspectives on each candidate if everyone asks the same questions?" There are two easy answers to this concern.

First, all of your interviewers bring their own biases to each interview and each candidate. *Interviewer perspectives on each candidate will be different because even identical answers are heard differently by different interviewers*. When we have tested highly qualified candidates going through multiple similar interviews, interviewers describe different outcomes and conclusions from their interviews. Much of this is due to different communication styles, in our experience. However, those differences are much more about cultural fit rather than significant divergence on evaluating core competencies for the role.

Second, as we'll learn in how to probe interview answers, *each interviewer will ask different probing questions and learn different qualities of each candidate*. This is again due to the interviewers' own experiences, personalities, and communication habits.

You don't have to allow your team members to conduct unprepared interviews in order to gain different perspectives on candidates. More prepared interviewers are better interviewers. The best preparation is predetermined questions designed to learn about each candidate's previous behaviors. Previous behavioral patterns are the most accurate predictor of future behaviors, which is what you'll be paying for when you hire someone.

17

The Basic Structure of Each Interview

IN ADDITION TO EACH INTERVIEWER using the same core set of questions, there is a most effective way to structure each interview they conduct. From the interviewer's perspective, there are eight phases, each explained in detail below. The phases will seem familiar to you and to prepared candidates. That's good—it eliminates the distress of interviewing anxiety. It helps unprepared candidates too—but it helps prepared candidates far more. That's good because we want to "spread the field" as we make our hiring choice. We want it to be as easy for us as it can be to separate the excellent from the merely good.

Introductions

The first thing to do in every interview is to introduce yourself to the candidate. Use both your first and last name. "Hi, I'm Mark Horstman" or "Hello, I'm Mark Horstman. Nice to meet you. Come on in and have a seat."

To really do this well, there's a best way to state your name. Don't say both of your names the way you always do. To you, it's normal, and you're good at it. You say your name fast. But to a nervous candidate, it's pretty darned fast, and often *hard to tell where your first name ends and your last name begins*. So do it right: Say your first name more loudly than your last, and pause between them.

So it's not: "Hi, Mark Horstman."

Rather: "Hi. I'm **Mark** . . . Horstman." Feel that full stop after your first name.

If you doubt this guidance, try it the next couple of times you introduce yourself to someone new in a social situation. *Accentuate your first name*. Then pause. Then say your last name.

On the other hand, the idea that forgetting your name is the kiss of death for a candidate is silly. Maybe he did, and he's forgotten, thanks to nerves. It's normal. Half of the human population isn't good with names. No job has as its primary criteria being good with names. This means don't take off your desk things with your name on them and then ask the candidate halfway through the interview, "What's my name?" This is embarrassing and unprofessional. If they forget, forgive them and tell them your name again, for heaven's sake.

The interview you're going to be conducting is so well prepared and comprehensive that if they're good at everything else, you'll be happy to forgive them their moment of forgetfulness. And if they don't do well, you won't need the gotcha of "they couldn't remember my name" to rule them out.

Surely you will have studied their résumés before the interviews, and you will know their names. But it's reasonable for them to respond to your introduction with their own names. [Haven't you introduced yourself to someone and then been a little surprised, even disappointed, when she doesn't respond in kind?]

After the candidate has responded, it's often helpful for each interviewer to say where he or she fits in the org structure: "I report to Mike Auzenne. I handle content and client relationships. I'll be one of your peers here."

You probably don't need to do this if you're the hiring manager and are the candidate's last interview. You can if you like, but he probably already knows. Remember, he started the interview day with you going over the schedule.

Last, in this introduction phase, thank people for coming in.

All together, it sounds like this:

> Hi. I'm **Mark** . . . Horstman.
> [Candidate responds]
> I report to Mike Auzenne. I handle content and client relationships. I'll be one of your peers here. Thanks for coming in today.

Candidates report that they respect and appreciate this standard way of starting every interview. As you surely have experienced, an interviewing day is a whirl of emotions. By the end of the day, every face has probably blurred together. The structured beginning resets the candidate and reduces the stress that's over and above what's helpful.

Brief Small Talk

Before you get into the meat of the interview, engage in some brief polite chit-chat with each candidate. Jumping right into what is your best first big question ("Tell me about yourself") is still a little jarring.

Ask some open-ended questions about the weather, their logistics, daily news, sports, or even the interviewing day so far. Note that we don't recommend asking yes or no questions. We're trying to establish a conversational tone. Starting with, "Good trip in? Good day so far? Did you see that the Dodgers won yesterday?" all engender short answers, and what will feel more like a questionnaire than a conversation. And if you start with yes/no questions after not introducing yourself, that begins to feel like an interrogation.

For instance:

How was your flight/drive in today?
What's the weather out there today/where you came from?
What are you thinking about the World Cup so far?*
How have your interviews been going?

Interview Overview

All of the above takes two necessary minutes to help candidates take a deep breath after their likely fears about making a good first impression. And, although this may help the unprepared nervous candidate, *it helps your best candidates even more*. They'll be relaxed and ready and be able to be conversational immediately. Even though the formal part of the interview may not have started, *you're still evaluating*.

Now you're going to give each candidate a brief overview of how the rest of the interview is going to progress. You'll tell them you're going to ask them a series of prepared, largely behavioral questions. You'll be taking notes and interjecting/probing for more information regularly. You'll also leave them some time to ask you questions, in most cases.

Here's a standard overview statement that is part of the Manager Tools Interview Creation Tool (ICT) output, which you can also find as part of the sample interview in the Appendix:

Thank you for interviewing with me today. Here at Manager Tools we use a behavioral interviewing style. I'll be asking you a series of questions about experiences you've had, and how you handled them. I've

---

* Regarding sports questions: You may not be all that interested, and may choose to not ask. That's fine. But don't avoid them out of a mistaken sense that sports aren't a professional topic. They are. Major sports results *are news, and are reasonable topics of polite conversation.*

got a series of about 10 questions. Don't be surprised if others here ask you the same questions in other interviews—that's normal. We want to be sure that each person we hire has the same qualities that have made us successful thus far.

There will be times when I interject to ask you for more information. Don't worry—that's normal. I will be taking notes. Please don't let it distract you. First I'll ask you my questions, and then I'll answer any questions you have of me. Then we'll finish up. I'm excited you're here, so let's get started.

Tell Me About Yourself

We recommend the first significant question you ask in every interview be "Tell me about yourself" (TMAY). It does several important things for a first major question.

Remember that this guidance is for everyone interviewing the candidate, not just you. If you did your own screening, you have already asked this question during your phone screen, and you may choose to skip it. Or you could still ask it as a natural ramp up to the bigger behavioral questions.

It's Easy

What could be an easier first big question than asking candidates to do what the entire interview is about—talking about themselves? That's at the heart of every interview (despite the Internet saying candidate prep should be about the company). Great candidates will have good, prepared, structured answers. Poor candidates will have thin answers and struggle with your probing about decisions and outcomes.

It Introduces the Concept of Probing

Typically, answers to TMAY will be higher level than a rote recitation of what's on the résumé. This means you'll be hearing more about career and professional decisions. You'll want to probe the "why" of those decisions. Candidates who will be good at making decisions on your team will be able to describe the options they considered, the pros and cons of each, and the process they went through to arrive at their decisions. Candidates who can't remember, or give simple "why" answers like "It seemed right at the time," "It was my only option," "I didn't really have a choice," "It's what everyone else was doing," and so forth, are sending a message that they don't have good decision-making skills. Even if a decision turned out not to have mattered, a candidate who can't articulate a decision-making process or paradigm won't be able to make repeated smart decisions working for you.

One of the problems with TMAY is the bad Internet guidance that so many candidates follow. The common guidance is that the best answer is "only one minute long, because the interviewer is only asking this in order to allow him to probe your answer. They know what they're looking for, so don't overdo it."

This guidance has crept into the mainstream because these would-be advisers don't know what a good TMAY answer is supposed to be. They know good interviewers are going to probe, so they don't have to have more specific guidance.

This is poor guidance. It leads candidates to appear unprepared and makes our work much harder in an interview. In many cases it means you cannot probe because the candidate doesn't say anything meaningful. Yes, you can work hard and unearth the decisions and outcomes that mattered, but it will usually take a long time. That means that you won't have time to get through enough of your more detailed behavioral questions *that are actually about the core parts of the job* so you won't learn enough to decide whether someone can do the job. Unfortunately, since our purpose is to find reasons to say no (and we don't have unlimited time), that means the poorly prepared (or advised) candidate is ruled out of our consideration.

[For the record, briefly, a good TMAY answer lasts three to five minutes. It gives a good overview with enough information to make probing around career/life decisions easy, but not so much that the answer is 15 minutes long, too detailed, and inefficient. You can learn more about our guidance on answering TMAY in our *Interviewing Series* of 50+ podcasts.]

It's worth noting here that time is a critical factor *working against all candidates*. Candidates who aren't prepared, who haven't studied their own backgrounds, and haven't practiced delivering answers to reasonably expected behavioral questions take longer to interview. If their early answers are poorly structured and we have to work harder to unearth what we're looking for, we will have less time to have all of our questions answered. Since we will probably run out of time without learning enough to say yes, we end up having to say no.

You might think, "Well, okay, that's an artifact of interviewing. With enough time, we might find them a great fit." You're right. They might be great.

But it doesn't matter: *You don't have the time.* It seems silly to us that so many managers aren't prepared with the right questions and don't have the time to study candidate résumés and take notes of interest, but then expect to have much more time to conduct much longer interviews.

Further, when we start taking more time *to find what we're looking for,* our confirmation bias starts to kick in, and we start to find it. Now we're trying to find reasons to say yes. *Reasons to say yes are always there, especially if a candidate has gone through previous screening steps.* This is violating the first principle of effective interviewing: finding a reason to say no. Never get so caught up in avoiding a false negative (saying no to someone who would have been a good hire) that you bring into play a false positive: Hell on Earth.

You might also say, "This is a communication problem." Again, you may be right. But usually it's much more one of lack of preparation, which surely is a good reason to have doubts about how much someone wants to come to work for you.

The problem with this mindset is that communication is the single most frequent behavior of all professionals. The inevitable result of thinking through communication skills and time limitations in an interview is that *someone who communicates poorly in an interview is going to be a poor communicator on your team*. Candidates know the limitations of interviews, certainly in terms of time. They know they won't be able to tell you everything. They know they'll have to highlight their best qualities relative to your job.

How many highly effective professionals do you know who would say, "Well, she is our best, but a terrible communicator?" That only happens with the rare genius whose role is usually specialized for him or her. That's rare enough to be beyond the scope of this guidance.

We have found that many managers think that the question, "Walk me through your résumé" is equivalent to TMAY. *It isn't.* "Walk me through . . ." rarely gives us any new information, which a prepared interviewer already knows. It also causes virtually every candidate to describe chronologically all or almost all of the jobs he's had, which, again, we already know. If someone has had seven or eight jobs, we're stuck listening to five minutes of things we already know. If you're interviewing a less experienced candidate, she doesn't have enough background to fill up the time she thinks is required for this answer. She then mistakenly start delving into specific accomplishments. This may or may not be relevant because she may be highlighting behaviors we're not interested in. That might be *interesting*, but it's inefficient because we may not have enough time left to find out whether she's done the things we want her to have done (and done well enough) to consider her.

Core Behavioral Questions Come Next

After you've probed through TMAY, move right to your prepared behavioral questions. Ask them in descending order of importance relative to the most important skills and abilities required in the job. We've talked about how to create them earlier.

Custom/Targeted Questions

You may have some custom questions (these can still be behavioral, following the three-part structure) you wish to ask. These may relate to your culture, your team structure or processes, or specific knowledge areas you wish to probe. We don't mean technical abilities here, generally. Technical evaluations—the most common today are in software development—are covered in separate interviews covered earlier.

Answering Questions

Once you've finished asking the questions above, it's appropriate to allow candidates to ask their own questions. Typically, candidates only have two or three questions.

If there's one portion of this interview structure that you can jettison in the interest of time, it's candidate questions. We don't recommend it, but it happens. Frankly, too often, candidate questions are unremarkable. If you have two or three minutes left at the end of the interview, asking for a question or two is fine. If you have five minutes, though, it may be smarter to ask another of your prepared behavioral questions or your custom questions.

Taking candidate questions brings into play the possibility that you have already made up your mind to recommend not hiring the person. If you've already made up your mind, *and you're fairly close to the end of the interview,* ask for candidate questions rather than asking more of your own questions.

Asking more questions (versus taking questions) holds a subtle danger worth considering. Once most interviewers have decided to say no, *we get sloppy.* Don't kid yourself: Candidates notice. It's off-putting to continue to field questions as a candidate when it seems fairly clear from the interviewer's demeanor (it's harder to hide and easier to see than you think) that he is no longer interested.

The way to avoid the sloppiness is either continue to ask your prepared questions *while still diligently taking notes* or, if you are near the end of the interview, take some questions from the candidate. But don't make the mistake of "resurrecting" the candidate who suddenly asks brilliant questions. Questions they ask are a lot less valuable than your comparison of their behavioral skills to the job requirements, which was what led you to that no recommendation.

If you decide to say no and then depart from your prepared questions, for far too many interviewers we've observed, that means you'll stop taking notes. Those are red flags for candidates.

Also keep in mind that we're only one person providing input during the Interview Results Capture Meeting. While we *generally* recommend an offer be made only to that candidate who receives unanimous yeses, that doesn't mean every situation is so clear-cut. It's better to keep your evaluation hat on, even if you've decided to say no. As we'll learn later, you're going to have to support your recommendation of not hiring with specific observed behaviors during the interview. The more behaviors you can cite, the more weight your recommendation will carry.

How to Evaluate Candidate Questions

There are impressive questions and not so impressive ones. But before we give guidance about how to evaluate them, it's valuable to consider the general idea of candidate questions.

Be warned: The vast majority of candidates think that interviewing is a "two-way street." Candidates have been told that their interviews are a time to learn about you and your team and your firm. This is true after a fashion, but it leads to more really stupid candidate Internet guidance. "Two-way street" and "learning about the company/job/team" become "the candidate is conducting his own interview," "the candidate is an equal partner in the interview," and "the candidate is deciding yes or no during the interview, too."

From the seeds of truth great lies are born. This guidance is often peddled by the same charlatans who encourage candidates to "answer questions with a question." But hey, *on the Internet, nobody knows you're a dog.*

Of course candidates are evaluating us as we are evaluating them. That's healthy. But the idea that this implies some sort of equitableness *as we are interviewing* is ludicrous. Candidates are *not* equal partners when we are interviewing them. If that were the case, they'd get to ask us as many questions as we ask them. Five minutes of a 75-minute interview is 6% of the interview.

No, *we* are in charge of the interview. We hold all the cards at this point. The candidate's evaluation of us is virtually meaningless if we don't make her an offer.

You'll note that we said "virtually" meaningless. It's completely meaningless for the candidate's relationship to this opportunity, which is why we're interviewing. But the candidate's sense of how she was treated certainly matters when she goes back to her current workplace or schoolmates and friends and has to admit she isn't getting an offer. If we haven't behaved professionally, or politely, or respectfully, she'll justify the lack of an offer with the interviewing version of Aesop's fable of the Fox and the Grapes, from whence comes "sour grapes": "I didn't want to work there anyway."

This is why we do so much to communicate in advance, explain what we're doing, why we're doing it, do what we said we were going to do, and make the candidate's logistics and interviews as pleasant as possible. It is really no harder to have high standards *while being nice about doing it.* Greatness in the workplace doesn't come from being so tough on decisions that you can be tough on people. Greatness is high standards gracefully achieved. As the saying goes about great managers: She can step on your shoes and still leave a shine. Be nice while you're holding people to high standards.

The kernel of truth about the duality of evaluation in the process is still true. The problem occurs when we or candidates think that those two evaluations *occur at the same time*. They do not.

When we're trying to make a decision, we hold the upper hand. Ninety-five percent of the work is about *our* decision. The candidate's decision only comes into play after we make an offer.

And then it's almost 100% his or her decision. In fact, among most serious interviewers, the concept of an offer is best summed up by the phrase, *when control passes from the company to the candidate*.

When the candidate does get an offer, his evaluation really starts in earnest. When we were evaluating, we were asking the questions. Once the candidate is in control and evaluating, that's the time for his questions. We'll talk more about that when we talk about closing the candidate whom we've offered.

All this means that the questions candidates ask during the interview are less important to our decision and to theirs.

Characteristics of Good and Bad Questions

Good questions show preparation, invite conversation, are related to the candidate's role, and ideally reference something discussed in the interview. Bad questions are questions about what the candidate will get or have in the role, or are not conversational.

Preparation   Off-the-cuff simple questions aren't prepared. Isn't it funny that interviewing is a "two-way street" and yet while you spent hours preparing questions, the candidate can get away with off-the-cuff questions? It's not funny, of course: It's embarrassing to the candidate.

A question that shows preparation alludes to the preparation in the lead-in to the question. For instance: "I noticed that demand is still strong for your legacy product. How will my role relate to the legacy product versus some of the emerging technologies?" "I've read that you're excited about new uses for your service due to legislation changes. How will the team's work be related to that, and how might that affect my work?"

Inviting Conversation   You've just finished asking conversational questions, interjecting, probing. For the candidate to then start asking yes/no questions, or questions whose answers are numbers is a miscue on her part. First (and you'll feel this when it happens to you) the conversational nature of the interview will suddenly die. It will significantly decrease the energy in the interview.

Further, yes/no/numeric questions (if they're truly going into the candidate's thinking about her interest) imply by their nature that there are right and wrong answers. This despite the fact that, in many cases, the candidate can't know whether supervising five or 10 people at your company is either a tip of the cap or a slap in the face. The behavioral interview questions you've just finished asking don't imply rightness or wrongness. They send a message that you're gathering a lot of subtle and complex interrelated information to inform an important decision.

Not About Company or Industry   [This guidance doesn't hold for positions—usually at the very top of organizations—where corporate strategies and factors *are part of the job for which the candidate is interviewing?*]

Candidates in 2019 (and for the last 10 years) have been told that their preparation should be on the company with which they're interviewing.

Much of that is in response to companies telling recruiting firms that they were tired of interviewing candidates who knew almost nothing about the job, and definitely nothing about the company. This was because they themselves knew that, thanks to web growth, there was information about their companies available easily to anyone. Before the web, getting information about companies took time and money that probably would have been better spent on preparation about oneself.

This turned into, regrettably, excessive preparation about high level corporate entities, strategies, competition, and business/

financial news *that had no relevance at all to the job for which the candidate was being considered*. That's what was easily available. Further, except for more senior positions (which take up a large percentage of the money spent on recruiting and interviewing and the majority of hiring news coverage), in our experience the vast majority of interviewees do not have nearly enough knowledge to be discerning about the answers they receive, because they don't understand them. And it's entirely possible they've asked someone who doesn't know enough to give a good answer. [This isn't a slight to someone below an executive-level role: Most directors (managers of managers) aren't privy to the product and profitability mix of the company by geography (as an example).]

Further, questions about company/strategy/industry are primarily to help the candidate decide how interested he or she is in your company. *This is a waste of time if the person does not receive an offer*. That makes it a poor tactical decision for the candidate. Every minute the candidate spends in an interview gathering information to make *their own* decision is a minute wasted on convincing the hiring manager about *our* decision.

Questions About Compensation and Benefits Are Selfish   Candidates who ask about how much they could be paid, what benefits are like, and how much time off they're going to have are making a similar mistake. Why does it matter *yet* what their pay is going to be when (a) we haven't decided to hire them and (b) we would be wasting our time figuring that out before the hiring decision is made.

All this said, you may wonder: Would we recommend not hiring a candidate based on poor or selfish questions? *Absolutely*.

There's no sense in engaging in any step in this process that doesn't help us make our decision. Remember that the first principle of effective interviewing is to find reasons to say no. We are prepared to miss a good candidate if our process does so in service of avoiding hiring the wrong person. Better to have a false negative than a false positive.

But because candidate questions are less valuable than candidate answers, it's reasonable to ask, What's the balance? We'll try to give guidance about this balance with two examples.

First, you have a candidate who, until he asks questions, is outstanding. He has great answers. He clearly has the right behavioral background in skills and abilities so that he could do the job. And he's a good or very good communicator. But then he asks a series of poor, and maybe selfish questions. Certainly, it's a letdown to what previously had been a good interview.

Faced with this dilemma, ask yourself: *Are his questions indicative of a selfishness or lack of preparation that I have already seen evidence of?*

Maybe his background *is* great, but you've had a vague sense of arrogance or self-centeredness during the interview. Or maybe you didn't sense it before specifically, but something was bothering you, and when you hear his questions, you're pretty sure there's a fit problem: He's going to be hard to manage or is not a team player. In this case, we'd probably tell you to recommend not hiring the candidate.

Or he has great answers, and there is not a hint at all of selfishness. You really like him and think he is a good cultural fit. In this case, it's probably reasonable to conclude that he has simply learned a bunch of bad interview preparation guidance and has asked bad questions thinking they are good (and they're not indicative of his character). In this case, we would probably suggest you recommend hiring him.

Second, you have a candidate who has done okay, but has not impressed you. Her answers were okay, but you had to work really hard in probing to get acceptable answers. You've probably concluded that her communication skills aren't that great. Then she asks a series of poor or selfish questions.

We recommend not hiring this person, in part based on her poor questions.

Regarding communication skills more generally: Remember that communication is the single most frequent behavior of everyone on your team. Poor communication skills are enough to not hire someone. Take, for example, the candidate who gives you a one-minute answer to a substantive behavioral interview question. You probe repeatedly to get at the underlying behaviors. *Then he or she answers every successive behavioral question with another one-minute answer.*

This candidate is not a good communicator, and we would not recommend you offer him or her the role. Candidates who have all the technical skills but not enough contextual and situational awareness to change how they communicate may get the job done, but will be weak team members.

18

How to Take Notes

TAKING NOTES IS SOMETHING people seem to find difficult at the best of times. We frequently are asked how to arrange notes in a notebook, what symbols or shortcuts we use, and how we find things again.

When it comes to interviewing, our notes become even more important. It's not because they're a legal document, though some people will tell you to be careful what you write because they are. It's because you need to be able to make a decision about whether to hire based on evidence. The only way to remember what you heard and what conclusions you drew is to have good notes.

What to write and where?

Pre-Print the Questions on Your Answer Sheet

If you use our Interview Creation Tool (see the Appendix), you'll have the ideal output: a pre-printed sheet with each of the interview questions, what to look for, and space to record your answers.

If your HR department uses competencies or standardized questions, they may provide you with a similar sheet. If no one has given you a set of instructions, and you don't want to license our ICT, you'll have to create your own sheet.

Why not just take notes on the next blank page in your notebook? You want to ask the same question in the same way every time. That's the only way you can be sure that you're comparing like with like when you review the answers from different candidates. If you ask one candidate "Can you tell me about a time when you influenced the direction of a project?" and another "How have you influenced project direction?" the answers aren't going to be comparable. Yes, the questions are similar, but there's a subtle difference. Judging candidates against each other when you've introduced subtle differences isn't fair. So however you take notes, you will need a separate sheet with the questions you're going to ask printed on it.

You could still use your notebook and a separate sheet. But that's two items, plus your pen and a coffee you're juggling, whilst you try to listen to the candidate and take notes. Why introduce the complication?

In addition, you might be asked for those notes six or eight months later or perhaps even longer. (There's some doubt about how long recruitment papers have to be retained in Europe, but the most common answer is six years.) If you had to go back and find one page in a notebook you were using a year ago, would you be able to?

Having each question and the relevant notes on one sheet of paper is easier logistically in the interview *and* for filing and retention afterward. (Filing it *with* a copy of the résumé and other candidate correspondence is a great way to look organized when asked for the documentation.)

Handwritten Notes Only

Note taking on a laptop has become quite popular lately. We here at Manager Tools are regularly told that we're Luddites for suggesting that taking notes on a laptop is almost always a poor choice, but we stand by our guidance. There are a number of reasons.

The most important reason is the purpose of taking notes: having a good record of what transpired. In other words, note taking ought to start with effectiveness and not efficiency. Studies have repeatedly shown that those who take handwritten notes have better recall (they score higher on tests of subjects presented) than those who take notes on laptops.

Our favorite example of note taking effectiveness involved three groups: laptops, handwritten, and a third group *who pretended to take notes with pretend pens on pretend paper. The laptop group's recall scores were the lowest of the three.*

There's even more to it than that. If you're taking notes on a laptop, your interviewee thinks you're doing something else, like email. It doesn't even matter if you turn off all other applications on your laptop: the interviewee will still assume you're doing mail, or messaging, or Slack. Surely this is enough reason.

And there's still more. Several years ago Manager Tools trained managers for a firm that sent researchers to interview patients in drug trials. They were thrilled finally to be able to deploy laptops to help with interviewing patients. Previously, they had to handwrite notes, then return to the office and enter them into their system. Laptops would allow more time in the field.

Alas, it was not to be. After a few months, they scrapped the laptop trial. Seems that the patients complained to their doctors that their comments/answers/feelings/symptoms weren't being adequately captured. As one of their managers put it to us: "They would talk for two minutes after we asked them a question, and didn't think that hearing only 50 keystrokes could be a faithful record of the exchange."

Often note taking via laptop is argued for based on efficiency. You don't have to take the time to type your handwritten notes to have them in your digital system if you type them to begin with. This is technically true, but off the mark. First, we can digitize all our notes by taking a photo of them with our phones and texting them or emailing them or posting them. No, they may not be 100%

searchable, but what are the chances that you're going to search for one word of an interview more than one or two days later? Zero.

Take your notes by hand.

Write Down as Much as You Can

While it's not fun to hear, our data show that one of the best predictors of those who are good interviewers (identifying true positives and true negatives) *are those who write down more of what the candidate said*. That's right—if you only gave us one datum to assess interviewers, we'd want to know how detailed their notes were from the interview: how many words they wrote down that the candidate said.

Of course, you can't write down everything. But as you know from taking notes, you don't have to write every word down to capture the key ideas being communicated.

Write Down Exactly What You Hear

This is the Manager Tools secret weapon against hiring litigation. It's also *much* easier for you as an interviewing manager. Write down exactly what you hear.

Many managers try to write down what they hear *and* simultaneously the conclusions they drew. So they might write: "Story about PM who lost control. Seemed to support manager & turned situation around. Good."

Here's why that's not what to do. First, your conclusions "good" or "bad" are written down in black and white. That's information for lawyers to twist if for some reason your notes should come up in litigation. There's a reason police statements are factual. The facts of what was said or done cannot be argued. The conclusions drawn can be argued. If your conclusions are not written on the page, they cannot be discussed. We promise you, if you take good notes, in the way we recommend, you will remember the conclusions you drew. We can from interviews we did ten years ago.

Second, it's much harder. Taking notes on a conversation is not a skill we practice much. Even when we're taking notes in meetings, we're generally taking notes on actions to be taken and things we need to remember. That's not the same as taking notes on what's said. Because we don't practice, we find it much harder when we need to do it. Trying to take notes on what's said, drawing conclusions, *and* writing down those conclusions are *three* things for your brain to do at once. Oh, and remembering to smile and nod at the candidate to keep her comfortable, think of your probing questions, and worry about keeping the interview on time? Don't introduce additional complexity to a task that is already complex.

Write down what you hear. You'll be able to take more comprehensive notes within the same timeframe if you just concentrate on this part of the task. For example: "Was deputy PM on 1M project. PM lost control & allocation tasks due to firefighting. C. stayed late one evening to update systems to provide accurate picture, talked PM through suggested task reallocation & supported at team-meeting when reallocation was briefed. Project on time & budget."

Even if you saw those kind of notes on a candidate you did not interview, you'd draw the same conclusion: "Seemed to support manager & turned situation around. Good." Now though, you know *why* the candidate is supportive and good, and so will anyone else who reads your notes.

Writing down what the candidate says is behavioral evidence of whatever recommendation you're going to make in the Interview Results Capture Meeting (IRCM), which we'll discuss in Chapter 20. You're going to have to make a recommendation of whether to hire or not hire the candidate, *and back it up with specific behaviors from the interview*.

If all you write down in your interview notes are conclusions, you won't be able to easily support that conclusion in the IRCM. If there are those in the IRCM who disagree with you, and they have supportive evidence and you don't, your recommendation won't carry nearly the same weight as your colleagues' recommendations.

Use Abbreviations

You do need your notes to be legible and comprehensible, but you don't need transcription-level notes. Depending on your industry and role, you'll probably have some specific abbreviations that you use a lot.

Removing the vowels from words is one way to make them shorter and yet preserve their meaning in most cases. We always use C. for candidate, as it saves writing the name when we need a subject for a sentence. For longer words, just use the first syllable: imp. for important and info. for information, for example.

Don't go too far though. If your notes look more like a quadratic equation than prose, you might be being too clever and making things more difficult.

Taking notes in interviews is something that managers want to make much harder than it is. Their fears over what's "required" for HR or in the face of later litigation drive them to erroneous conclusions. It's easy. One sheet of paper with the question and space to write notes. Write down what you hear. File with the résumé. Done.

19

How to Probe Behavioral Interview Answers

THE QUESTION WE HEAR MOST frequently from managers is "What questions should I ask?" This is a fine question—and that's why we license our Interview Creation Tool. But it's not the best question.

The best question is *How do I evaluate answers?* Most of us do this poorly for all kinds of reasons. We over-rely on our guts. We haven't prepared well enough to know what we are truly looking for. We believe "We'll know it when we see it." We like answers that sound like our answers. And on and on.

But let's go back to first principles. What are we looking for? A person who can do our job well. What is the raw material that allows someone to do a job? Behaviors.

So we prepare behavioral interview questions, and then we ask them. And then, unfortunately, candidates don't answer with behaviors! They have reasons, for example, most can't imagine they have enough time to go through all of their behaviors in something like a project they're discussing. They're right. Also, many candidates have not professionally prepared for a behavioral interview by knowing how to highlight their behaviors as they describe one of their accomplishments.

What this means is we have to ask our questions, listen to the answers, and then *probe for behavioral details*.

This is not to say that any time in any answer we're going to probe for more information on anything the candidate did. It would take too long. (We hope you're seeing that as full an evaluation as we're wanting to do, time is our enemy.) We can't probe for everything. That's why we did our advance work to highlight the most important behaviors relative to the job for which we're hiring.

Asking behavioral questions and then probing for behaviors is the best balance interviewing science has come up with to both (a) give us a broad overview of the candidate's experience and (b) the opportunity to dive deeper into those areas that are important to us.

Before we talk about what to probe *for*, though, we need to learn *how* to probe.

When we probe, we're taking the candidate off of his or her narrative. And because we're going to be probing quite a bit, we have to avoid giving the impression we're constantly interrupting.

What this means is that when we probe, we start with an apology. Remember that we're trying to make the interview conversational. That helps the best candidates be at their best, and it helps all candidates relax and describe their experiences positively.

And when we interject in a normal conversation, we naturally make some brief apology for the break.

All Good Probes Start with an Apology, and Then Ask for Additional Information

Now that we know how to phrase a probe, what do we probe on, or for? As a general rule, there are two areas to probe into: (a) decisions candidates make and (b) the most important behaviors we have identified in our preparation.

We probe decisions because candidates who have made good decisions in the past will make good decisions for us. Good decision making is something that doesn't get talked about very often when it comes to interviewing, unfortunately.

We understand the thinking and have used it ourselves. No sense hiring a great decision maker to design a building who has never designed a building, right? But there's a missing bit of analysis here. Decision making is an inherent part of any skill. Peter Drucker would remind us that decision making is a behavior, because it includes not only the choice we make, *but the actions we take to implement the choice*. If we don't probe decisions candidates have made, we won't learn whether they have good decision-making skills.

Decision making is one of the key building blocks of one's ability to act independently, to learn, and to grow one's skills. If we want to hire directs who can function independently, and if we want them to be able to do more in the future, we have to know about their ability to make decisions. And the only way to do that with any reliability is to ask questions about how they have done so in the past. Probing on past decisions is a classic use of the fundamental principle of behavioral interviewing: Future behavior is best predicted by past behavior.

So we want to know more about candidates' decision-making abilities. How do we know when to do this, since probes aren't prepared like our core questions? It's simple, really: *We're going to listen for situations in their answers where we think they made a decision.*

In our experience interviewing surely tens of thousands of candidates over the years, we've learned that there are some words or phrases that candidates use that suggest a decision was made.

- **"So . . . ," "So I . . . ," and "So then I . . ."** When someone says, "so," there's an implication that a cause and effect has occurred. We want to know "Why?"
- **"It was obvious . . ." and "obviously . . ."** This is a case where the candidate is using a form of verbal shorthand. Usually he's not trying to not tell us his thinking (though that's sometime

true). But it could be a time for us to interject to understand why it was "obvious." In what way is it obvious?

- **"I concluded" and "I came to the conclusion . . ."** Conclusions imply some form of reasoning. What was the decision process?
- **"My plan was . . ."** If the outline of a plan is shared without giving some overview of the options considered or the plans she didn't choose, it's time to ask about those. How was the plan created? What options were considered and discarded?

There are some trivial situations where you probably don't need to jump in for elaboration. For instance, "He said it was okay to move forward, so I continued with my plan." In this case, the rationale for the continuation of the plan is stated beforehand.

Unfortunately, with decision making, too many of us start with the idea that "the inherent if-then implied is obvious or explained . . . ," and we don't ask for clarification. A big part of the reason for this is *we assume the candidate used the same logic we would have to have taken the action he took*. This is wrong half the time—if not more.

One of our favorite examples came interviewing a recent college graduate. After mentioning he chose the quite impressive college he chose (and where we were interviewing) and his other (also good) options, we asked how he came to his decision. He said, "A couple of my friends were going there."

That's not an indicator of good decision-making skills. Yes, we would forgive this due to the inexperience of youth. But it was a reason to probe further on other decisions. It provides an interesting comparison to another graduate who laid out her choices, talked about their relative strengths and weaknesses, and chose the school that fared the best against her key criteria.

Here are some examples of full probes—apology and query—to understand a candidate's decision making:

- "Go back quickly, if you would, please, and explain your reasoning there. Why did you choose that action/plan?"

- "Sorry to interrupt here, but tell me more about how you came to that decision."
- "Excuse me. Why did you decide to do that?"
- " Sorry, go back. Why that course of action?"
- "I apologize, but can you help me understand your analysis. Why those choices?"

Probing about decisions isn't hard. It's just something most of us don't do. We're too busy thinking about a particular skill we need, whether it's creativity with new media, or closing customers, or queuing theory, or cost-efficient structural design.

But for all of those skills and abilities, decision making is a critical underlying factor. And rest assured: The group of candidates who can talk about *why they did what they did* is the group who knows how to make good decisions. If you have poor decision-makers, you may end up making all of the decisions for all of your directs all the time.

Probing for a Critical Behavior: Communication

We strongly encourage you to make communication skills one of the core behaviors you interview for in virtually all cases. Communication is the most frequent behavior all professionals engage in at work. Without good communication skills, a team member reduces the effectiveness of his team, almost regardless of their strength in other skills, even critical ones. Not only is his work not fully utilized when he communicates poorly, but he creates more friction among team members, which reduces performance overall.

One of the classic mistakes in modern interviewing is finding a great technical talent, and allowing the candidate's technical skills to overshadow weak communication skills. It almost always ends in regret.

We've learned a few clues that suggest a needed probe to learn about a candidate's communication skills. There are many, because we communicate so much at work. These should point you in the right direction:

- **"I talked with/to them."** This seems obvious, but most candidates assume we don't want every conversation reviewed. They're right. But in some cases, we do. Often, we want to know whether a candidate can change how she has a conversation based on what she knows about the person she's talking to.
    - *"Excuse me, but to go back a bit, what did you say? How did the person respond? How did you convince him?"*
- **"We had a meeting, and . . ."** Meetings are all about communication. And they're different than one-to-one conversations. A meeting may imply group discussion, a presentation, voting, acquiescing to someone else's idea. Perhaps the person did advance work socializing the idea or recommendation.
    - *"I'm sorry, could I just ask what happened in the meeting? How did you present your ideas? Did you have a ready presentation? Did you know how everyone felt beforehand?"*
- **"We exchanged emails . . ."** Email is a significant part of professional life and communication. But email is also only one of our choices, between internal chat boards, face to face, meetings, text messages, Slack, reporting, etc.
    - *"Sorry, tell me more about that, about the exchange. Why did you choose email? What other choices did you have? What is your usual criteria for choosing email?"*

Listen for these cues and others, and make communication one of your screened for critical behaviors. The more you interview, the better you'll get at it, and the more you'll realize what a difference it makes.

SECTION
5

Deciding and Offering

20

Interview Results Capture Meeting (IRCM)

USUALLY, WE DON'T THINK OF opportunities to speed things up as also increasing the quality of the output, but the IRCM does just that.

The IRCM is almost as important as the interviews themselves. It happens after everyone has finished their interviews of each candidate. Don't wait until *all* candidates have interviewed if more than one has made it to your final interviewing day. Remember that candidates are not being compared to the others: each is being compared to the standard you set in your preparation.

The IRCM's purpose is simple: to capture all interviewers' recommendations for each candidate—in as short a time as possible after the interviews are complete. When you ask other managers and associates to interview one of your candidates, you tell them, based on when the interviews are, when you will have the IRCM.

Meeting Logistics

As a general rule, hold the IRCM the day *of*, or the day *after* a candidate's interview day. We recommend keeping them to 30 minutes, but often you need an hour, so schedule an hour, and if you finish early, so much the better.

147

Agenda

You start, taking five minutes to remind everyone of your agenda. Then give each attendee five minutes to report. We don't recommend allowing open discussion after each interviewer's recommendation and justification. Just let them all get through their reports, and *then* allow open discussion. The agenda is:

0:00—Welcome/agenda
0:05—Report 1
0:10—Report 2
0:15—Report 3
0:20—Report 4
0:25—Report 5
0:30—Open Discussion
0:60—Close

We know there are some readers who are thinking it's hard enough to get people to interview your candidates—how are you going to get them to interview *and* come to another meeting? The answer is simple. Mention a couple of less than great hires, tell them how the new person will be supporting what *they* do in their areas, tell them that you'll always be available to help them with *their* interviews, and tell them, finally, that once they see the meeting in action, they'll want to do it themselves, guaranteed.

All Interviewers Attend and Report

Everyone who interviews comes to the meeting. It's normal for some people to have a conflict. When someone can't attend, our guidance is to have the person report in an email to the hiring manager by the time of the meeting. Have everyone follow the "What and Why" guidance in the next step.

Use the "What and Why" Method of Reporting

When each interviewer reports, whether in person or by email, he or she covers two points: what—whether to hire or not hire, and why—behavioral support of the recommendation.

First and foremost, they recommend **hire or no hire**. Just that. Nothing fancy. If you've interviewed, whatever you talked about, you *start* with the Hire/No Hire recommendation. **This is critical.**

Interviewers are going to want to talk about their experiences, about something specific that was said. There are interviewers who want to avoid making a decision, and some who want to avoid disagreeing with the hiring manager. They want to defer to you. But the whole point of multiple interviewers is gathering different points of view.

To be clear, you *don't* start an IRCM with an open discussion. Interviewers who know this will happen find it easier to come to the meeting *without a hiring recommendation*.

Note what the IRCM structure causes: every interviewer has to finish the interview with a decision: a hire or no hire recommendation.

An interview is not "a discussion." An interview is not "a chance to gather information." It is not a chance to "get a feel for a candidate."

An interview exists for each interviewer *to gather the information necessary in making a hiring decision*. An effective interview results in a recommendation to hire or not to hire. That's the result/outcome/product of interviews. Not information, data, thoughts, or feelings that will then be bandied about as "the group" come to a decision.

The format of the IRCM forces every interviewer to interview with the purpose of making a decision individually about the candidate.

Without the requirement to decide after the interview, interviewers end up just gathering data. When that happens, our testing shows that the biggest determinant of the hiring decision is *who talks first, loudest, and/or most.* This isn't a professional way to assess talent.

Without the IRCM structure backing up the interview as a decision, whomever talks the longest and loudest wins. Ludicrous.

So the first words each interviewer says at the meeting are "Hire Her" or "Don't Hire Him."

Then they *support* their recommendations based on what they saw and heard in the interview. Again, we **urge** you to require recommendations *before* support. Interviewers want to talk about what they saw, what they heard, how it was interesting, what clever conclusions they drew. But none of that matters **nearly** as much as whether they recommend hiring or not hiring.

When giving their "why," interviewers support their recommendations with behavioral examples in four areas: *Interpersonal, Cultural, Skills, and Technical*. (You only provide technical input if you're qualified to share it, usually because you conducted the technical interview.) If we're interviewing a project manager in an IT organization, and you're the marketing person with whom she must have a good relationship, you're NOT going to give feedback on the technical details.

For each of the three or four areas, you use the What and Why format:

- **Interpersonal:** How well did he interact with you. What did he say and do?
- **Cultural:** How well you think she would fit with the firm. What did she say and do?
- **Skills:** What did you see in the answers to the four behavioral questions, including how the answers were communicated, and why do you say that?
- **Technical:** How did the person perform in the technical assessment?

In each case, the "why you said that" brings up a specific answer or behavior from the interview that shows competence in each area. This helps managers look for those very things in interviews.

Here's an example of an interviewer report:

> I recommend we don't hire Andrew. Interpersonally, he kept interrupting me . . . even **after** I asked him to let me finish the question. Culturally, I have concerns as well. He said twice that collaboration was overrated—that he believed in leaders deciding. Skill-wise, there's no question he could do the job. He told me about his success bringing a difficult project in on time. But the interpersonal and cultural areas are **big** concerns. I say no.

After everyone else, you, the hiring manager, share your recommendation.

Deciding Whether to Make an Offer

Now that you have heard from all of the interviewers, you have to choose to put into action whatever decision model you've chosen. Many managers use some form of voting process: a majority or a super majority. Some managers even consider everyone else's input to be only input, rather than recommendations, and the hiring manager's interview and opinion take precedence over all else.

We recommend having a (modifiable) standard of unanimity in your decision. *If everyone recommends hiring the candidate, including you, prepare to make an offer.*

This, of course, means that Manager Tools recommends *not offering* someone who doesn't receive unanimous support from your interviewers. There are situations, though, which make this not an ironclad rule.

Perhaps you have one or two interviewers who are relatively inexperienced, and their input reflects that. It might be reasonable to overrule their recommending not hiring someone whom others with more experience want to offer. Perhaps you have someone who hasn't followed your process, either in the interview or in the reporting during the IRCM. You might choose to ignore that input.

If your team all recommend not hiring, but you disagree, we'd recommend you not hire the candidate. Otherwise, it will come to be seen that your vote outranks all the others combined, and all but the most professional and experienced teams are likely to be less diligent in their support of your process.

The decision model we recommend is off-putting to managers who have never used the Effective Hiring Process before. Typically, input after interviews is not required to be structured. It may not be timely. Different interviewers notice different things (because they asked different things, based on differing concepts of the role and different levels of training).

We have found that the divergence and lack of structure most managers have previously experienced will almost completely disappear if you follow the Manager Tools Effective Hiring Process. Trust the process. If, after everyone reports their recommendations and support, you're uncertain what to do, thank everyone for their input and adjourn to ponder your decision.

Because ultimately it is your decision.

How to Decide When Interviewing Multiple Candidates

At this point, it's usually time to make an offer decision. *You make an offer decision even if there are more candidates to interview.* The reason for that is you can't be certain that the other candidates will come in. Also, remember that this process compares candidates to the hiring standard, not to each other.

If you do have other candidates to take through the final interview day, and your current candidate warrants an offer, you simply delay making the offer to the candidate at this point. Depending on how long it is until you get to the other candidates, you'll want to stay in touch with the candidate until you've made a final decision.

This brings up a special note about the hiring manager's interview with each candidate. It happens last, so you (the hiring manager) have the additional responsibility of telling each candidate what the process is going forward. We encourage you to share how you capture results in the IRCM. Tell them that you will be in touch on a regular basis (usually every three days) until a final decision is made.

If after your first final interviewing day you decide that your candidate meets your standard, *you could still choose to make an offer to your first candidate without seeing the others*.

This is a hard concept for many managers. Usually that's because we're used to the idea of comparative interviewing, and waiting to see everyone and then "choosing the best." But that's also usually because we don't set clear standards for hiring and compare candidates to that standard.

You will find that comparing candidates to a prepared standard makes hiring much better and much harder. That means that when you find someone who meets the standard, you'll want to make an offer to the person *even if someone better might come along*.

21

How to Check References

Before we make an offer, we have to check references. We are amazed at managers who don't do this. And you have to get as much information as you can, in a world where many companies limit their disclosures. Here's how.

We check references between "I'm ready to make an offer" and "I will make an offer to this candidate." When we check references, we are essentially saying, "I've decided, and now I'm going to do one last check to make sure I haven't missed anything." The chances are slim that there will be anything there, but no sense in not spending an hour or two just to eliminate any later regrets. Plus, if everyone learns that we always check references, that reduces our future candidate risks.

We don't check references to find out why we want to hire someone. We check references to make sure there aren't concerns we haven't uncovered ourselves.

1. Start with an Admission and Factual Questions

Over the past 20 years, companies have grown less and less willing to be open with those checking references. This is absolutely an overreaction to defamation lawsuits of 25 years ago, and a trickle down of executive employment contract law.

If you've heard that "companies don't give references anymore," that's true, sort of. If you ask someone official at a firm, particularly in HR, there's a fair chance you'll get someone who spouts the company line at you. "We don't give references." This is simply lawsuit avoidance . . . though when was the last time you heard of someone suing a firm for defamation in a reference?

But some managers who aren't aware of the rules (and who don't refer you to HR) often still do answer reference-seeking questions. **They may feel they're not giving a reference, but they're still telling us stuff we want to know.**

They probably know something of "I don't have to do this" or "I think I'm not supposed to do this." But there's a way to go about it that will get us some good information.

The first rule is start with an admission and factual questions. This is what HR has probably told them, or that they have surmised: "We can confirm dates of employment." They've actually probably told them more, like what they really can't talk about, but most managers miss some of the detailed guidance. And, remember, this is only in companies that have HR orgs that are legally careful. The vast majority of firms aren't as careful as that.

So for any reference checking, we start with factual questions that help the manager or reference see that we're not asking for too much. Further, we're going to say at the outset, "I only have a few questions. This won't take more than five minutes." But first, we admit that the interview process has progressed to the final stage, and we are simply checking references. It would sound very much like that:

- "Our firm has been interviewing Allie Simpson. She's done well, and we've reached the point where we do a simple reference check."
- "We've been interviewing Allie Simpson, and we're in the late stages, where we check references."

*If we don't tell them it's in the late stages, or give some indica-
tion that the candidate has done well, references are much less
likely to be candid about weaknesses or concerns, because they
won't see themselves as messing up the candidate's chance for a
fair shot in the interviews.*

Most companies only go to the trouble of checking references
at very late stages, if they do it at all. Some, in fact, make offers
before checking, but make them contingent on a successful reference check. Why, then, they don't *tell* the reference that is beyond
us. When a reference hears an offer has been made, he is much
more likely to be open with concerns. And to be clear, remember
our first principle of interviewing: **The Purpose of Interviewing Is
to Say NO.**

One more key: *Always tell references that you're calling because
they were listed as a reference by the candidate*. This makes them realize that they've been asked a favor by the candidate, and they're just
doing that favor by talking to us.

2. "Would you please confirm the dates of employment?"

The first question is a no-brainer. This question even the most
hardened of companies tells managers they can answer. Companies allow this question to be answered to provide themselves
with the opportunity to police those people who would list them
as a part of their employment history when in fact they never
worked there.

Therefore we **must** ask this question first, to make sure the most
basic of assumptions is checked. If there is a noticeable difference
in the dates of employment, after multiple interviews, this could be
(and by us **would** be) a serious breach of ethics that would result
in declining to offer. There are exceptions, but dates are often
"fudged," and the rationale for a "mistake" would have to be com-
pelling if the mistake worked in the candidate's favor.

The fact that we start with this question helps references understand that *we* understand the situation *they* are in, and helps them get comfortable with us for later in the discussion, when we're definitely going to ask questions that possibly they're not supposed to answer. To be clear, and as we'll repeat later, we will not imply that they should answer any questions, nor will we behave disrespectfully or rudely if they don't. We're simply going to assume both that (a) there may be rules in place that limit them and (b) they still want to help the person who put them down as a reference. (Wouldn't you, when you're listed as such?)

If you're talking to HR, don't give them the dates you've been given. Ask them to look them up. *That* is validation. They may not have it available, or at least say they don't, but usually they're willing to find it, even in places where referral policing is done.

One more thing about HR: If you're talking to HR, and you get through all of these questions at a large well-known employer, you are either an exceptionally good relationship builder, talking to an easy mark, or talking to a reference who really loves that candidate. It's probably all three, and well done.

If you're not talking to HR, and the manager you are speaking with doesn't have access to records, you may have to suggest the dates and accept confirmation rather than independent validation. That's okay.

3. "Could you confirm the job title for me please?"

This is another simple factual question. Many companies tell their managers that "you" (the manager) can't talk to them, but "we" (HR) can. There are legal reasons for this. And they tell managers that in addition to the dates of employment, they—HR—will also confirm what the job title was.

In our case, we're asking for two reasons. First, we want to know the actual job title. Remember now, we still haven't made an offer, and we're looking for reasons to say no. Sadly, very few people believe that references are checked, and job titles are often doctored. Second, we want the reference to still feel we are asking questions that he or she can't get in trouble for answering.

To be clear, a job title that is not an exact match is not grounds for significant concern. There is enough lack of clarity within firms themselves that sometimes there is some wiggle room. There are enough subtleties that we could suggest guidance just on the kinds of differentiation we think are reasonable.

As a general rule, the bigger the company, the more clear job titles are. And there are certain titles that mean certain things.

A couple of discrepancies that would catch our eye:

- **Use of Manager Without Directs or a Budget.** These are **not** dispositive, but "manager" implies one or both of these. Yes, we know that there are individual contributors who are legitimately called manager, and they don't have a budget. We would recommend concern is indicated if there is a pattern of discrepancy.
  - This guidance still stands in the event that someone uses "manager" when the reference says "team leader" or "supervisor." It is a judgment call, but "manager" implies more responsibility in most places, and it's reasonable to expect a professional to understand the distinction.
- **Use of Director While Not Supervising Managers.** Director has a broader, less precisely defined usage, and so we would be more broadly flexible here. But "director" generally does imply manager of managers. Again, a pattern is a red flag; this by itself is perhaps unworthy of scrutiny.
- **Larger, Known Company with Patterns of Discrepancies.** The bigger the company, the more carefully titles are managed. Any pattern of difference there would seriously concern us.

For all of these situations, if there were a discrepancy between the title given and the one the candidate has used, it would be completely reasonable for you to share what was on the résumé or said in the interview, to give the reference the chance to say something like, "Oh, yes, well here the terms manager and supervisor are interchangeable." This isn't a great answer (and you may have to assess, unfortunately, the truthfulness of it), but it is one that we would probably counsel giving the benefit of the doubt on if it were the sole discrepancy.

This is again a case where the question does not **give** the job title, but asks the reference to say it first. This is the difference between validation, which is what we want, versus the more passive "confirmation."

4. "Please comment on the accuracy of the following job description."

Notice here that we're still talking basically about facts—a job description. But now we're asking for comments. The core of the question stays benign, but we're asking for elaboration by asking for a comment.

In this case, we read the job description from the candidate's résumé. [Obviously, for a job of which the reference in question would have knowledge.] This gives some wiggle room, because we don't require candidates to precisely reproduce the official job description. That's also why we ask for comments. In our experience, references understand this.

In the majority of situations, the reference makes some comment about the description being basically true, **but then comments in some other way that is helpful also**.

If a reference up until this point has been fairly tight-lipped, you can ask this question in two parts to increase the chances of a more meaningful elaboration. The first question would be a purely factual one. For instance, "The job we're considering Allie for will have a budget of X. In his job description, he states that he managed a budget of Y. Is this reasonably accurate?"

Once you have an answer there, it's easy to simply expand to the entire job description. "Let me just briefly read you the job description and ask for your comments." This tends to get a little more openness. [Obviously a discrepancy in the budget that wasn't a rounding error would be noteworthy.]

5. Always Be Thankful to Build Rapport

This probably goes without saying, but we're not expecting gross discrepancies to be commonplace. If someone has made it through the entire interviewing process—a tough interviewing process— you should have discovered already if he's willing and able to mislead in a printed document intentionally.

Therefore, it should be easy to be verbally thankful for every answer we get. We want the reference to relax. As often as is reasonable without sycophancy, say thank you, and express appreciation for the time and any candor shown beyond purely factual answers.

6. Then Progress to More Substantive Questions

The questions we've asked up until now have been potentially helpful, but again we hope that big discrepancies would not occur because that would indicate you haven't been able to see the candidate's apparent willingness to mislead.

We hope that through simple, benign questions, and answers responded to with thankfulness, that the reference has relaxed enough that we will receive more expansive answers to more substantive questions.

Nevertheless, at no time must we ever express frustration or disappointment with references who hew tightly to a narrow answering of the questions. That will destroy any trust we've built, and it's just not professional. It's completely appropriate for them to be loyal to whatever guidance they've been given, and we have to assume that not being open is in service to a higher value than helping us or the candidate who listed them.

7. "I was told about Project X. Can you confirm his involvement?" followed by, "Can you tell me about the results?"

This is a two-part construction designed to smooth the transition from facts to opinions, from surface to substantive. In this case, you don't have to make it about a project, but rather about anything specific either discussed or stated on the résumé. The bigger/more important the project, the more likely you're going to get a good answer, because the reference thinks you're validating the scope of his involvement, rather than his strengths and weaknesses, for example.

The results part will often be assumed by the reference as validation of whatever the candidate has told you, whether he has told you anything in detail or not. The question transitions the conversation from facts to depth.

8. "What was his best contribution?"

This is asking for information about our candidate's strengths, or a significant accomplishment. At this point, we hope, the transition from validating facts to sharing insights has been made.

It does happen that you'll have a reference who will stick to the party line. If so, there's nothing wrong with asking this question, knowing full well you won't get a good answer . . . and, you never know. Maybe at this point she'll remember she was chosen to be a reference, and she's supposed to help the candidate. Usually, though, references are willing to be open at this point.

9. "What would you say his areas for improvement are?"

This question has to follow the previous one about strengths or best contribution, because they come as a pair so often in interviewing. In most cases, the approach we've outlined here works quite well, even with legally minded managers, and you learn some new information despite it being perhaps "against the rules" to share it.

This is not to say that you're going to learn something bad: If you're a good interviewer and have followed a professional process, it's unlikely that there will be some dark revelation. But in light of our purpose, to say "no," the fact that it's possible you will learn anything of concern justifies the effort.

10. "We are looking at him for _____ role. How would you assess that fit?"

Once references have relaxed enough to answer the previous questions, if they have, this question asks them directly to apply their wisdom and insight to help you "assess" something. Very few can resist the call to their ego here. And once they engage their assessment hat, they're unlikely to be perfectly positive.

The negatives are what we're hoping to hear. We don't expect to hear anything that on its own is a knockout punch, but four or five negatives in the same vein, if they are in an area where strengths are called for in your role, might be enough to cause you to pause.

11. "If you were me/us, any concerns about employing him/her?"

I've always hoped that here anyone I asked to be a reference would scoop up all the negatives he or she **may** have mentioned in the earlier answers and say, "Regardless of any of my answers, you'd be a fool not to hire him." But once you've asked for assessment in the previous question, you shouldn't be surprised at the willingness to be what we call in recruiting "dumb honest": saying something true that could be damaging if taken in isolation.

Managers who check references get better at it and learn what works and what doesn't. It's best to have a standard approach, which time and experience will cause you to modify for even better results.

22

How to Offer

NOW THAT WE'VE FINALLY FOUND someone worthy of an offer, let's follow a process and create an offer that they'll accept. There are all kinds of chances for stumbling at the end, but be smart, do it well, and you'll end up hiring the best candidates who have multiple offers.

Some managers don't know that sometimes HR wants to be the one to make offers. HR is often evaluated on the numbers of offers they make and how many are accepted, as part of recruiting metrics. A lot of managers mistakenly turn over making offers to HR when they don't have to.

Letting HR make your offer is the ***single biggest mistake managers make when offering***. At this critical moment, it's not a good idea to turn over to someone else the only step you have left. It makes no sense at all.

Never turn this job over to HR. If HR is making offers, it's because someone before you made a mistake, and/or some lawyer thinks it's better this way. Lawyers don't run your company, managers do. HR doesn't run your company, managers do. Don't turn over the seminal step of how your company grows—improving its talent base—to a lawyer or HR.

And, we're not against HR here. Many HR managers do this well, better than managers. But that doesn't mean we managers can't learn how.

Just think about turning over the act of making an offer, and then hearing from HR, "Well, he seemed interested enough. I can't quite put my finger on why he declined your offer." What if HR doesn't know to leave a detailed offer message? What if they mess up because they're not completely familiar with your special area? These is a delicate moment for you as a hiring manager.

Even if it's policy to have HR make the offer, *go ahead and make the offer first.* Yes, you're reading that right. Tell the candidate you're going to have HR call after you, to do it "officially" and to go over details, as part of the process. Ask him or her to accept to HR, officially.

After making your "early offer," call HR and tell them you're ready for them to call the person. Tell them you've already "teed up" the candidate and she's ready to accept.

Do Some Prep Work

This is of course different for every company—and this is why HR gets involved often. Start by asking HR what comprises an offer. Ask for the benefits information for the position you're filling.

Do not make an offer based on salary and deadline alone. **Know the key points of medical, dental, insurance, vacation, flexible benefits, pension, and incentive pay.** Take your time, and take some notes as you prepare, because you want to appear knowledgeable and confident. You need to know more than a laundry list, but you don't need to know every monthly deductible *yet*. Find out *who* you're going to refer questions to regarding benefits and compensation.

Consider Increasing Parts of the Offer

As you're preparing the list, see whether there are any parts you want to and *can* increase. The one that often allows some flexibility is vacation for exempt employees. You *can* increase it . . . many managers give team members additional time off for various reasons.

Why **not** tell them they can have an extra week? And that you're flexible on time off when necessary?

There may be other benefits as well, based on your company. Read them through as you're preparing.

Make the Offer the Moment You're Ready and You Can

We don't know why some managers delay. Everyone has been on the receiving end of a delayed offer. *Don't do this to your candidates! Make your decision, do your prep work (if you haven't already), and MAKE THE CALL. (There are exceptions, discussed later.)*

If you can, do it from a landline. Clear your desk. Turn off your mobile. Turn off your computer monitor. If you can, do it in the morning—that gives the candidate extra time, and you will sound better and feel good the rest of the day, rather than going home and wondering what the candidate is going to do.

Furthermore, she may accept immediately, and then you have time to take action *that day*. Or, if she declines, you can take action *that day*.

Don't Wait to Make an Offer in Writing

Make your offer verbally. It's faster, it's more personal, and it drives faster decisions.

Your organization may insist on creating a written offer letter. They may even say that "nothing's official" until the offer letter has been signed and returned. That's fine; you can still get a verbal acceptance and start the onboarding process right away. The chances that someone accepts verbally and then shortly afterward declines in writing are so small that you won't have wasted much work. But more importantly, you will be much more likely cementing a relationship with someone who will be working for you soon.

It's Okay to Leave a Voicemail

We don't know who started the guidance that leaving an offer via voicemail isn't a good idea. It's comical how it happens: telling someone to call you back but not telling him why. Phone tag for three days, all the while with the candidate not knowing whether it's good news or bad, though perhaps assuming. In our experience, the vast majority of candidates assume it's negative. Then the manager says, "It's good news" and the candidate now sort of "knows," but starts worrying about details. This is crazy.

Leave the offer on voicemail or an answering machine. Have your notes ready to do so.

Be Upbeat; Don't Forget Praise and Congratulations

This is a huge missed opportunity for most managers. Take a moment and sell. Talk about fit; talk about your desire to hire the person. Tell him how high your standards are, and how hard they are to meet. Talk about things he did during the interviews. Talk about accomplishments he's had. Praise him.

Some folks will say that this will increase the chances that offerees will think they deserve more money. That's not our experience. Candidates want to be *accepted*. They want to be *wanted*. Downplaying the joy of an offer to decrease the possibility of negotiations is like cutting off your nose to spite your face.

The Five Components of an Offer

An offer has five components: Offer, Position, Compensation, Start Date, and Deadline.

Offer

You start with the word **offer** in the first sentence. Don't say you'd **like** to make an offer. Say, "I am excited to make you an offer."

Position

Tell the candidate what position you're offering. This is usually straightforward, but sometimes new positions become possible based on the candidates' interviews, or they were being looked at for more than one position.

Usually, position includes location. This is also usually straightforward, but it's good to be clear.

Compensation

Compensation includes both base and incentive pay, as well as benefits associated with the role. Managers often forget to mention vacation/holiday/paid time off (PTO) when offering.

Some of these items may seem rudimentary. We nevertheless encourage you to give details. The fewer reasons you give candidates for asking questions, the fewer doubts they will have as they consider your offer, *and the more likely they will be to accept.*

Start Date

Tell the candidate the earliest you would like him to start, and that you're open to discussing it because of his logistics. If there is a "no later than" date, state that also.

Share Your Deadline

Offers always include deadlines for the offeree's decision. As a general rule, we suggest giving a deadline about one week from the time of the offer, and the week almost always includes a weekend. If you offer on a Tuesday, you could state a deadline of the next Monday. If you're making the offer on a Friday, you could ask for a decision by the following Friday. Except in extreme cases, allow the offeree one weekend between the time of the offer and the deadline.

If you don't give a deadline, your offeree isn't obligated to answer. *This means that if you make your offer without a deadline,*

you can't make another to someone else until the first offeree declines.
This is an untenable situation for you and your organization.

In the event the candidate doesn't say yes by the deadline, technically the offer expires. Technically, you don't need to do anything if you don't hear from a candidate. But with all the work you've put into this process, and the high standards the candidate has met, we encourage you to contact your offeree a day before the deadline (in addition to whatever other communications you have been making) to assess his or her thinking.

Yes, it is professionally somewhat rude for an offeree to wait until the last minute to accept or decline. But the offer is theirs until the deadline, and the alternative (no deadline) is even worse.

To be clear, there is a concept in offering that the definition of an offer is not just its components. The idea of an offer is *when control passes to the candidate.* Keep this in mind as you make your way from offer to decision.

Finally, it can be reasonable to offer an extension of your deadline to a candidate. It would be extreme in most cases to offer anything more than one extra week. And it wouldn't be unreasonable to offer less than that to a noncommunicative candidate who asks for that much or more at the very last minute before your deadline. As we'll discuss shortly, you'll be communicating with the person in the interim, which should virtually eliminate the chances for surprise.

Finally, if something changes in your assessment of your offeree, you can choose to rescind an offer. It would probably have to be something fairly significant, but it happens. If your offeree's behavior changes notably, it's painful to consider rescinding, but it may be necessary.

Regardless of all these various scenarios, remember that you're the hiring manager. This is an offer for someone to come to work on your team. Don't let HR take control of your timing or have some unclear-as-to-its-origin "policy" drive your timing.

Ask for Acceptance

Don't be afraid, also, to ask your offeree to accept your offer right when you make it. Make it clear they don't have to. Don't pressure them. But it's a great way to start a relationship if they do. Imagine telling your team in a group text message that your offer was accepted on the spot, within an hour of your IRCM.

Put it all together—it sounds like this:

> "Matt, I'm *thrilled* to be calling to make you an offer. I'd love for you to come work for Manager Tools. It's very hard for us to find people who meet our standards, and when we do, we're eager to have you join us. Our discussion about new products *completely* fired me up.
>
> "The position is as we've discussed, coaching associate. The base compensation is $80,000. Incentive pay in the form of bonuses and commissions is up to 40% of base. You'll be able to live wherever you want, based on our discussions. We have a pretty liberal scheduling policy. You have unlimited vacation, unlimited sick days, unlimited personal days. If you want it, you can take it. The medical and dental plans are as we've discussed. If you have any questions, we'll get them all answered. My cell number is:___. My office number is ___. My home phone is ___.
>
> "I'd like to have an answer by next Monday, the 27th. I'm also eager to have you accept now if you're ready. Will you accept?"

Make Yourself Available for Questions

You'd be surprised how many folks seem to think it's time to leave the candidate/offeree alone to decide. This is silly. You want to be able to influence the candidate's thinking because her brother-in-law who works for the government might be influencing her too, and he doesn't know a **thing** about your job. In fact, what's worse, he **thinks** he knows a lot and wants to tell her about it.

Share your mobile number, and offer to take calls at your offeree's convenience.

Make HR Available

Of course, make HR available. Give them the candidate's name, a phone number, and an email address. Ask your HR business partner to reach out proactively to make it easier for the offered candidate to ask questions.

But also make sure they know *you* are the primary point of contact. You can say it like this: "If you have *any* questions, please just call me. If it's benefits or HR related, I will find the right person to help you if I don't know the answer."

Don't turn over all benefit questions to HR. They don't have the sense of urgency that you do . . . and you have to be on top of the candidate's thinking and timing.

Keep Other Candidates on Hold

This is covered in detail in Chapter 24.

Call Every Three Days for an Update

You may only have to do this once, or maybe twice, but gee whiz don't just let the lines go dark. Pick up the phone and ask, "Any questions? I'm eager to have you start and want you to make a good decision."

23

How to Decline

FOR CANDIDATES WE'RE NOT GOING to hire, the last step in our hiring process is either to tell them they're not getting an offer or to let them exist in a frustrating limbo of not knowing what their status is. Here's how to do it right.

You're Obligated to Notify a Candidate of a "No" Expeditiously

As with so many of our managerial choices, we ought to ask, *How would we want to be treated if we were on the receiving end of this process?*

Everybody we know says the same thing: *If you're not going to give me an offer, I want to know about it, and as quickly as is reasonable.* Job candidates all say that if there is a reasonable chance they could be considered, they want to stay in the running. But if they're not going to get an offer, if they're out of the running, *they want to know about it right away.* It doesn't do them any good to keep thinking about your opportunity. The candidate needs to be freed up to think about other opportunities.

So, the standard is simple. When we know we're not going to make an offer to a candidate, we're obligated to communicate quickly that he's not going to get an offer. As quickly as is reasonable. And we can think of no situation that would justify a manager not making that phone call **the day the decision is made**.

You Can Wait for an Acceptance Before Notifying a Declined Candidate

Let's say two candidates (or more) did well enough to justify being considered. You decide to offer Candidate A. Simply because you're going to offer Candidate A doesn't mean you have to turn down Candidate B yet.

This situation doesn't contradict our first rule, because we haven't decided to rule out Candidate B yet. We don't know we are not going to offer B simply because we have decided to offer Candidate A. If Candidate A declines our offer, we may choose to come back to Candidate B. So we don't rule B out yet.

Once A does accept, your next call has to be to B. But until then, if B is still in it, you can wait.

You Can Rule Candidates Out Before You Make a Hire

That example aside, of course we don't have to wait until we get an acceptance to decline a candidate. Remember: We don't interview to pick the best candidate. We interview to determine whether anyone meets our standards for the job. Only if we have more than one candidate "above the line" do we "choose" whom to offer.

So if a candidate doesn't get above the line—and remember also, *the purpose of an interview is to rule someone out, not to help us hire*—we expeditiously turn her down. **We don't wait until the process is done to tell a candidate she's been ruled out. The moment we know we're not going to pursue a person, we tell her so.**

Be Direct and Simple When You Inform Them

This is where so many managers go wrong. The first mistake most managers make is never letting someone know. They leave the candidate in limbo. *Just because this was done to you doesn't mean it's the right way to do it.* Don't visit this mistake on others after you hated being on the receiving end of it.

When the decision is made, make the phone call quickly. That's right, *you've* got to *call*. You can't decline a candidate by email. And if you can't decline by email, you sure can't decline by text message or instant message or direct message or Facebook post or any other medium. Phone call, period. Here are a couple of examples of how it might sound:

> Roberto, I'm calling to let you know we won't be making you an offer. There was a lot I liked about our interactions. But we have decided to choose someone else who was a better fit for us. I know this isn't good news, but I also know you wouldn't want me to wait. I wish you well in your search, and in the future.

> Camille, this is Mark Horstman. I'm calling with less than great news, unfortunately. We won't be making you an offer. You're not a fit for us right now. I wish you well in your search, and hope you land in a great place.

You'll notice that neither of these calls has any chit-chat. **Do not start the call by chatting briefly.** If you can't make yourself not do that, about as far as you want to go is to say, *Roberto, how are you? . . . I'm well thanks. And, unfortunately, I'm calling to let you know . . . Or, Camille, Mark Horstman. How are you? . . . I'm fine, thanks. I'm calling with less than great news, unfortunately . . .*

The moment most candidates hear it's you, they are expecting news. This makes them nervous. After a couple of back and forth comments, the air is heavy with portent. And when you're calling with a declination, they're going to think that you were dreading it and extended the chit-chat to avoid saying they were out, which will make many feel you're not confident enough of your decision to not feel guilty about it. Don't make the drama any worse. If you can, avoid the chat altogether.

And because searches are associated with some sense of urgency, you *can* leave a voicemail for a candidate. You'll know this the first time you try to leave a message for a candidate that doesn't indicate what their status is. "Hey, Roberto, this is Mike Auzenne. Give me a call," is surprisingly hard to do when *you* know what the outcome is, but you don't want them to know. Even worse, try exchanging several voicemails with a candidate who is out of the running but doesn't know it yet. You'll hear increasing anxiety in his messages to you and increasing frustration. It usually ends poorly.

There are many who think that leaving a voicemail is cold or callous. We disagree. Job searches have an inherent urgency. But the sting of a decline justifies the humanity of a call, and not the cold urgency of a text or email—let alone a boilerplate in either media.

Here's how a voicemail might sound:

Patricia, I'm calling to let you know that we won't be making you an offer. I know that's hard to hear in a voicemail, but I thought it was better to give you the information quickly rather than risk playing phone tag or sending an email. You have a lot to offer, and unfortunately, you're not a fit for us right now. I wish you all the best in your search.

If you don't leave a number, or don't suggest a return, usually there will be an assumption that you don't need or want a call back. If you are willing to offer feedback—which we will discuss in a moment—then leave a callback number or suggest the person return your call.

If someone does call back, *let the first call go to voicemail*. This allows you to assess the response to your declination. If the person is respectful and appreciative, politely asks for feedback that you're willing to give, or just wants to say thanks directly to you, feel free to call back. If the message suggests that you're unlikely to have a good call with the person, you're not obligated to return the call.

[We are aware that a voicemail creates the possibility that someone will see a message from you and play it for others, hoping for good news and to share it. It is ludicrous to suggest that this faux pas is the responsibility of the caller. All voicemails are assumed to be for the private use of the recipient. This is not a reason to not leave a voicemail.]

You Can Offer Feedback, But You Don't Have To

Typically, there is no requirement to give candidates feedback about how they did or why you didn't hire them. There are good reasons for this. Many seasoned managers will tell you that they have tried and have received incredulous responses indicating that the hiring manager is *wrong, they **do** have that skill. Or that's not what really happened, and besides it was a silly question anyway.*

If you don't want to offer any feedback, and you are asked, simply respond:

That's not something I do, unfortunately. Hiring is a tough choice. It's often a subtle choice. The distinctions between candidates are ones of degrees of ability, and the degrees are often very small. It's not as simple as one person is good and the other is not. So I've found communicating well about the distinctions to be virtually impossible. You have a lot to offer, and we just don't see a fit right now.

They'll be stunned to silence by that answer, usually.

But . . . We would make the case that in some circumstances, you can trust a candidate enough to provide some comments.

Here's our guidance:

Say, "You didn't demonstrate . . ." This phrasing is simple and effective. And you don't have to say "demonstrate." There are other constructs that are fine. Here's how it sounds:

- "Bob, unfortunately you didn't demonstrate effective presentation skills. That's not to say you don't have them or that you can't develop them."
- "You did not demonstrate mastery of the analytical tools necessary for high performance." [Mastery is a word often referred to in interviewing and reviews.]
- "There was not enough evidence in your interview of strategic thinking."
- "You didn't demonstrate the requisite skill in marketing planning we're looking for."

The point we're making is a careful one. We're only saying that a necessary skill or behavior or ability **wasn't used in such a way that was visible**. It's simply a representation of what has happened. **We're not saying the candidate didn't have it, we're saying he didn't show it.** When we say "demonstrate," we mean, "you didn't do or say." Demonstrate means to show or exhibit or express.

No one who supports the concept of behavioral interviewing or unbiased performance communications would argue with the standard being **demonstration of a skill or ability or behavior**. One of the beauties of the system of demonstration of behaviors is that it protects all of us from the vague systems that intentionally defy accurate description, **often thereby supporting the improper or unethical evaluations of people based on their inherent characteristics. If a standard cannot be behaved against, or if the standard is not behavior or demonstrable, it can be used to deny opportunity to effective performers due to characteristics beyond their control or in the minds of the evaluators.**

These comments don't suggest a lack of potential. Nor are they an attack on the person. There are so many ways to talk about someone not meeting a standard that are clumsy and not effective. For instance:

- "You just don't have it."
- "I'm not sure you're cut out for this."
- "I don't see it in you."
- "You may not be the right kind of person for this job."
- "I think it's out of your reach."

These are all essentially false and arrogant things to say. What's more, they're characterizations of the person or of future ability. *It is hubris for us to judge someone personally or dismiss his potential based on an interview.*

A lot of managers say these kinds of things. It's easy to feel powerful when you choose who will be hired. It's easy to feel powerful when you get to make decisions about who receives the biggest raise. But it's the effective manager who humbles herself at these times and stays within the bounds of professionalism, by commenting only on demonstrated behaviors.

We don't judge people. We compare their demonstrated skills against a standard our organization sets and that we bring to life. The best way to communicate *not judging* is to stick to behaviors and what was demonstrated.

This is the right way to do it. It's simple and professional. And we ought to treat our declined candidates as well as we would want someone to treat us.

24

How to Handle Two
Viable Candidates

WHAT DO WE DO WITH two viable candidates? When we've found two candidates that we'd be willing to hire, both of whom are "above the bar," how do we handle the candidates?

Communicate Personally and Directly with Both Candidates

As hiring managers we have to be the one who communicates with candidates at this point. Too many managers outsource part of their communications with offerees/candidates. We communicate with the top candidate, and then we don't communicate with HR regularly about the status of the second candidate, allowing there to be a gap in our knowledge of the situation.

The process of offering and closing ought not be outsourced. The efficiency value of allowing others to communicate is far outweighed by the loss of effectiveness when we're not the ones doing the communicating. HR will never understand your needs, or your timing, as fully as you do. And they will *always* add more time to the process. Increased time with decreased value makes little sense.

Don't allow someone else to have a conversation and then either (a) not tell you about it or (b) characterize it for you. This characterization will lack some of the subtlety that you will be able to hear because no one else understands your situation or the candidate as completely as you do.

We talk to all candidates. If we reject someone, we tell him so. If a candidate is still pending, we tell her so. If a candidate has questions, we're **happy** to take those calls. What if HR flubs an answer and you lose someone over it?

Immediately Communicate to Both That the Decision Is Pending

We've finished the interviewing process, and we've gathered input from the Interview Results Capture Meeting. Out of that, we learned there are two candidates who meet our overall standards. This means we could see ourselves hiring either one of them.

What now? Before we communicate rejection to those candidates who didn't make it, we have to quickly call those candidates who are still viable.

We must communicate that the decision is still being made, and that they are still very much in the running. Some candidates have been ruled out, but they are still being considered due to their strong performance, and decisions like this one take time.

Here's how it might sound.

> Roberto, we were *very* impressed during your interviews. I'm calling to let you know that you were highly recommended, and we are trying to come to a decision. Some candidates have been ruled out, but you are still in the running. Sometimes it takes several days to get all the details worked out, but I will be in contact in

the next few days to keep you posted. Congratulations on your performance.

Note that this statement is made to **both** of the remaining viable candidates. This isn't the statement we make to our "top" candidate, because we haven't decided who our top candidate is yet. Right now, we're just being open and providing more feedback than most organizations do.

Here's another example:

Claire, I'm calling with good news so far. You did very well in your interviews, and you are still in the running. We've eliminated some candidates, and we're still very interested in you. Sometimes these decisions take a few days, and I didn't want to leave you hanging. I will be in touch as I know more.

Also note the beauty here of **not** having made a decision in terms of whom to offer. By communicating **quickly** and **not** about your decision, you avoid being in the awkward position of being asked if someone is your first choice, which you would rather not share.

Please do not think that the solution is to communicate quickly to your top candidate, in hopes of a quick decision, while saying nothing to others still in the running because you don't know what to say. Too many managers do what has been done to them, and communicate too little. It's one of the reasons all of us hate this process—it's being done wrong, for the wrong reasons.

Shortly Thereafter, Offer the Top Candidate

Once we've made our decision, we offer the candidate we have ranked as best. When we have multiple candidates, we must move quickly. In this situation, taking longer than 72 hours to make a decision between two candidates is too long.

Frankly, unless you intend to ask for more information—you have all the information you're going to have. We recommend sitting down and deciding. We think if you want to, you can do it *in one evening*. No two candidates are that equally matched, and your delay is likely, in our experience, to be indicative of a lack of interest in offering, not in deciding *which* of the two to offer.

Provide a Short Decision Deadline to the Top Candidate

Remember that every offer includes a deadline.

In this situation, we recommend that the deadline you set is **by 5 p.m., 4 days from the start of the day you are making the offer on, or by 8 a.m. Monday if that deadline falls on the weekend**.

If you offer on Monday, even if it's Monday at 4 p.m., the deadline is Thursday at 5 p.m. If you offer on Tuesday, the deadline's Friday at 5 p.m. If you offer on Wednesday or Thursday, the deadline's Monday at 8 *a.m.*, and if you offer on Friday, the deadline's Monday at 5 p.m.

We've found these deadlines are not ill-perceived by the candidate waiting in the wings. For once, historical slowness, the lack of crisp processes, the lack of clear communication that every other hiring company goes through actually helps us. Our viable candidate whom we haven't offered is going to consider this delay reasonable, and will not assume that he is being "passed over for someone better."

Communicate Every 72 Hours to Your Second Candidate

Just as we communicate with the candidate we offered every 72 hours, so with our second candidate. After 72 hours too many candidates' active and negative imaginations get the best of them. It's so easy to remain in the front of candidates' minds by simply touching base.

It might sound like this:

Cedric, I just want you to know we're still working on things. We feel we'll have an answer for you shortly. I suspect it will be by [insert one day past the deadline of the candidate who has been offered here]. I'm sorry for the delay.

Only Allow 1–2 Day Deadline Extensions

We're not big fans of deadline extensions. It's completely reasonable to say **"no"** to such a request. And if you feel the request is based on a fair reason, grant the request but limit the extension to one day, two in unusual circumstances.

But remember: The primary reasons candidates give for delaying decisions is uncertainty about fit . . . and waiting for another offer to come in. Don't assume yours is the only offer someone is considering.

If Your First Candidate Accepts, Reject Your Second Candidate

If your first choice accepts, be thrilled. And **quickly** call your second candidate and decline them, as discussed in Chapter 23. The fact that we have held this person off in hopes of offering him or her means once we know we can't offer, we have an obligation to close the loop quickly.

If Your First Candidate Declines, Offer Your Second Candidate

If your first candidate declines or can't accept by the deadline, it's time to offer the second candidate. No mention is made of the first candidate and that offer, in the same way that this offer and other offers are private matters.

In addition to following the normal offer process we recommend, we might begin with, "Allie, I'm thrilled to be calling you with an offer. Sometimes these things take time, and I apologize for the delay. I want you to know how excited we are, and we're hopeful that you'll join our team."

Perhaps all of this seems pretty simple, and in a way it is. But we've seen too many managers handle this poorly by giving short deadlines or failing to stay in touch with the second candidate. Doing things well is worth it after the expense and investment of a process that brought us two viable candidates.

SECTION

6

Onboarding

25

Onboarding New Hires

Well done! you've set a high bar, you've prepared, screened, and interviewed; someone has met your standard, and you've made an offer. We hope your offer is accepted. This part of the process feels different doesn't it? After all that work, it's uncomfortable, and maybe even frustrating, that we're no longer in control of our fate.

That feeling is a sign that you've started the Manager Tools Onboarding Process.

It might surprise you that we're talking about onboarding already. Most organizations think of onboarding as what happens once a new hire starts work. It's about administration, HR, and security.

But that approach is strategically flawed (in addition to being inefficient and ineffective). Here's why. If you think of hiring the way most organizations do it, there's the process of interviewing, and then, if someone accepts, there's onboarding once they arrive. There are two quite different phases, separated by the time between offer and start date.

*This approach is the way it is because those are the times when **the organization is in control of what's happening**. The entire time between offer and start date is left out of most hiring guidance and onboarding, because the company isn't in control from offering to start date.

But there's a far better way to think about, and do, onboarding.

Looking at it conceptually, hiring someone is really just about *organizational continuity*. The organization needs work to be done to support its mission of serving society. Conceptually, then, *filling that need for work is all part of the larger process of continuity: from work not getting done to that work getting done again.*

What most of us think of as the hiring process (mostly interviewing) is really itself just part of the organization's *continuity* process.

What most of us do now is think about interviewing and onboarding because that's within our control. But the more strategic and professional approach is to see all of it as part of organizational continuity. If we're part of a continuity process, everything we do is to *minimize the amount of time when work's not getting done.*

That means taking responsibility even when we're not in control: after we offer, and after they accept, right up until the start date. The best way to do that is to lay to rest the idea that onboarding is about admin.

Onboarding is the part of the organizational continuity process where, after we find the right person, we minimize the time before he or she is fully effective. With a continuity mentality, there are only two phases in our efforts: finding the person and making the person effective.

With the continuity mindset, when we make an offer, it's not time for us to "stop working" and "start waiting." That feeling reminds us that now our job changes from finding the person to maximizing his or her effectiveness.

That's onboarding. Here's what to do.

The Phases of Onboarding

It's one process, but there are different emphases as the offeree/new hire/employee moves through it. Onboarding may last nine months or only three months. Regardless of the length, there are always five phases: close, welcome, prepare, admin, ramp.

Because onboarding is much more organization-specific than interviewing, we can't make precise recommendations that will work for 90% of the managers 90% of the time. Most managers though, come up with a quite serviceable list of tasks from their own memory along with some emails asking for input from peers, HR, IT, Security, Finance, Accounting, and others.

After we cover some guiding principles, we've also included a sample of the Manager Tools Onboarding Checklist, available to our licensees. Even if you're not a licensee, the sample image will give you a basic template for how to construct your own unique checklist.

Close

First we **Close** the candidate. We have to communicate with him in ways to help him want to accept. We regularly communicate, potentially with multiple folks on our team involved. Offerees must never go more than three days without someone reaching out to them. We respond quickly to requests and questions. We arrange communication with others.

The more often we communicate, the faster they will become efficient, the more likely we will be able to build a strong relationship, and the more able we will be to divine when there are problems.

Welcome

Once they've accepted, we **Welcome** them. Multiple people reach out and stay in touch regularly throughout the period from acceptance to start. Perhaps there is a site visit, or a house-hunting trip, or even work to be shared.

Prepare

While we're welcoming them (but mostly after), we **Prepare** them as much as we can for their first days. There may be admin that can be done in advance. Again, there is often work that can be shared in advance, or at least background on the work that we do. There are often concerns about security here, but don't assume that security prohibits any communications about work status and progress or programmatic updates.

Too many managers assume that nothing can be shared with accepted hires who haven't started. Make sure that *is* the rule before shutting them out by not allowing them to ramp up early. And don't assume that someone saying, "I'm not sure you can do that" is an order not to. It's probably seditious for many managers to hear, but if you are sharing work stuff to your home email address (because you're not the CIA or Mossad) you can probably share it with someone else's home email address.

Admin

Probably shortly before the start date, and certainly for a time after, we take care of **Admin**. Most managers think of admin as being what onboarding is about. It's certainly important—you can't work without a badge and some forms filled out, and you can't get paid if you don't work. Admin is necessary. But it's not sufficient.

Ramp

The last phase, which overlaps admin, is **Ramp**. Ramp is what's important about onboarding. It can actually start earlier than admin, in some ways, but it becomes the clear focus in the early days after the new hire's start date. Certainly, things learned earlier—even during interviewing—could be useful during ramp.

Ramp comprises activities to accelerate your new hire's performance improvement. It assumes most admin is done, so as to allow full working abilities and authorities. Ramp is where all the support staff usually melt away, and it's your job as a manager to "make the new guy useful fast."

Discipline Makes Learning Possible

This tenet of management isn't limited to onboarding, but it's especially true of it. Because onboarding can be episodic (this is one of the reasons so many of us don't have processes or checklists) and yet important at the time, it falls again victim to Horstman's Christmas Rule.

If we don't have a process, we're making it up as we go. That means performance is mixed, outcomes are harder to predict, and causes of success and failure are harder to isolate.

But the discipline of a known, communicated, and followed process—even a first-time, incomplete, known-to-be-missing-something one—helps us learn. We know what we did. Even if we inadvertently skip a step, at least we know we didn't do it.

So we're going to write it down. We're going to publish it internally. Nothing wrong with sharing it with candidates, so they can help us. And because it's an important, persistent process, we're going to hotwash it every time we finish following it. (If you don't know how to do a hotwash, also called an After Action Review or AAR, *There's a Cast for That™*.)

Switch from Weaknesses to Strengths

A simple but important concept in Onboarding is that once you've made an offer, *you're no longer looking for weaknesses*.

Think about the purpose of interviewing: to find a reason to say no. If you can't find a reason to say no, take a step back and look for reasons to say yes. If you do say yes, the ayes have it, and the nays lose the vote.

Part of the value of saying no in interviews is to "build a high wall" around your organization. Every new hire must be as good as or better than your organization. Otherwise, you're hurting the organization. But it also sends a message to those inside the wall that high standards are being applied to their potential future colleagues. This shows respect. What's more, new hires who make it over the high wall are more likely to be trusted and respected earlier by their new colleagues.

Sure, as a manager you're always evaluating the strengths and weaknesses of your team. You'll notice errors and add them to your evaluation of a new employee. But that won't be your focus. If it is your focus, if you continue to focus on weaknesses or problems, you'll communicate that to others. That will hamper your new employee's ramp speed and damage his early relationship efforts.

Once someone has accepted, she's over the wall. She's on the team. Maybe she's new, but she's no longer a candidate. Maybe she hasn't started, but she's on the team. And hey—be careful about referring to the new hire as, "the new guy or gal." It will last a lot longer than it will be useful. All you're doing is creating a pseudo-probationary period. How does that help build trust?

Communicate and Report

One of the benefits of a documented process is greater ease in communicating status and reporting progress. Also, because of the effect of the Christmas Rule (see the Introduction to this book), sometimes a documented process helps team members remember what they're supposed to be doing.

Perhaps most of all, you as the manager are responsible for all of what's going on, but you can't possibly be trying to do it all yourself. If others are involved in the onboarding (which of course they are), you ought not have to ask them continually whether they've done what they're supposed to do. A smart spreadsheet (or Smartsheet) or whatever project tracking software you use (not so full-featured as to be off-putting to rare users) should work. And it wouldn't be out of the question to have the new hire update the reporting system on a daily basis.

All this allows each onboarding experience to be tracked. And *that* is exciting, because now we have data about how the process worked.

And that means we can do a professional hotwash in no more than 15 minutes. If we're clever, we make decisions on the spot, and we have someone editing the process live during the meeting on a TV/big screen so all can contribute. (Maybe on your first run-through.)

Onboarding is the hiring manager's responsibility. It's not complex. It just requires discipline and some basic tracking and reporting. It's not enough to get someone to say yes to your offer. You've got to help the person to be effective. That's the whole point of an effective hiring process.

The Manager Tools Onboarding Checklist

For our Licensees at Manager Tools, we created a customizable spreadsheet that lists over 250 editable tasks that cover the gamut of onboarding responsibilities. All you have to do is enter your offeree's name and, as you have them, their acceptance and start dates. It lists in chronological order all the tasks you might conceivably need to onboard someone in virtually any situation.

Once you have the list, you can easily go through it and delete tasks that don't apply to your situation and add tasks with their own deadlines. Every task has a due date associated with the timeline. If a task is not yet due, that cell shows white, with the due date. If the task is due in the next few days, the cell shows orange. When you type done in the field, the cell turns green. And if the task is overdue (the date is in the past) that task's status cell shows red. The moment you open the document you can tell the status of all the tasks.

As an example, Figure 25.1 shows the Spring 2019 hiring of Sandy Churchill.

#	Phase	Calc Date	Days	Tasks	Due Date
				Offer To Acceptance	
1	Close	Offer		Make offer	done
2	Close	Offer		Ask Sandy Churchill whether she has all the information she requires to make a decision	done
3	Close	Offer		Inform Sandy Churchill of deadline for acceptance (not more than two weeks)	done
4	Close	Offer	3	Call/Email/Text Sandy Churchill for an update. Any questions? I'm eager to have you start and want you to make a good decision. Remind her of the deadline.	21 Apr 19
5	Close	Offer	6	If Sandy Churchill declines at any point, probe for reasons	24 Apr 19
6	Close	Offer	9	Call/Email/Text Sandy Churchill for an update. Any questions? I'm eager to have you start and want you to make a good decision. Remind her of the deadline.	27 Apr 19
7	Close	Offer	9	If Sandy Churchill declines, probe for reasons	27 Apr 19
				Acceptance to Start	
8	Welcome	Acceptance	1	Confirm start date with Sandy Churchill & enter it into the start date cell on line 7 (you can put a placeholder in here if you're not sure yet)	4 May 19
9	Welcome	Acceptance	1	Notify your boss that Sandy Churchill has accepted	4 May 19
10	Welcome	Acceptance	1	Notify HR that Sandy Churchill has accepted	4 May 19
11	Welcome	Acceptance	1	Ask HR if there have been any relevant process changes if it is more than 60 days since your last hire	4 May 19
12	Welcome	Acceptance	1	Notify Sandy Churchill of her HR point of contact	4 May 19
13	Welcome	Acceptance	1	Notify your team that Sandy Churchill accepted and her start date	4 May 19
14	Welcome	Acceptance	1	Ask your team if there have been any relevant process changes if it is more than 60 days since your last hire	4 May 19
15	Welcome	Acceptance	1	Notify IT that Sandy Churchill accepted and her start date	4 May 19
16	Welcome	Acceptance	1	Ask IT if there have been any relevant process changes if it is more than 60 days since your last hire	4 May 19

Figure 25.1   The Onboarding Checklist for a new employee

Even if you create your own spreadsheet/task list from scratch, you're far better off keeping track of all the myriad tasks yourself than either turning them over to others or wondering every day what still needs to be done.

Hiring isn't just interviewing. Effective hiring means helping your new team member achieve high effectiveness as fast as possible. Planned and measured onboarding is indispensable to that goal.

Afterword

YOU MAY FEEL LIKE THERE'S too much here to try to do everything we recommend the next time you hire. We recommend you do as much as you can. If you have to start somewhere, and have to pick just one thing, develop behavioral interview questions. Then use those when you interview each candidate.

Then, next time, do better phone screens, and ask two or three of your directs to conduct interviews similar to yours using your predetermined behavioral interview questions. Next time, add the Interview Results Capture Meeting.

All that said, you *can* do all of this the next time you hire. No, you won't be great at any of it, but you'll learn fast. And if you interview two, three, or four people, when you're done you'll be a hell of a lot better hiring manager than 95% of the managers in the world.

The first few times you use this Manager Tools Effective Hiring Process, conduct a hotwash to review what went well and what you need to take a look at to make it better next time. If you don't know how to do a hotwash—also called an After Action Review or AAR, *There's a Cast for That™*.

Hiring is the most important managerial practice.

197

Acknowledgments

I'M INDEBTED TO MY WIFE Rhonda for tolerating the extra work this book has been, on top of all my regular work at Manager Tools. She was the first to read the manuscript. She said it was good, so it must be.

Many thanks to all of my colleagues at Manager Tools. What we do is special, and it's great to have special people to do it with.

Special thanks to my business partner Mike Auzenne. I'm blessed that you run things while I'm busy thinking and writing. Beat Navy, partner.

A special note to my colleague Wendii Lord, who leads our Career Tools podcast. Wendii is especially knowledgeable about hiring, and I leaned on her for research and editing. I used the raw material from many Career Tools podcasts in this work.

Finally, thanks to the Manager Tools community of listeners, Licensees, clients, and customers. We're downloaded three million times a month these days. Some of you have been listening to us for 14 years. We take your commitment of time to learning from us very seriously. I hope this guidance serves you and your organization well.

About the Author

MARK HORSTMAN IS CO-FOUNDER of Manager Tools, a management consulting and training firm. He is also co-host of the Manager Tools podcast, the number 1 business podcast in the world, with over three million downloads a month. Virtually all of the Fortune 500 are clients of Manager Tools, including Apple, General Motors, and Salesforce.com. The firm trains thousands of managers throughout the world every year.

He is also the author of *The Effective Manager*, a bestseller on Amazon. He is a graduate of the United States Military Academy at West Point. Following his service, he worked in sales and marketing at Procter & Gamble. He lives in Pebble Beach, California.

Appendix

POSITION: Administrative Assistant   INTERVIEWEE:

DEPARTMENT: INTERVIEWED:

CREATION   Jul 30, 2011
DATE:
INTERVIEWER:

INTERVIEW GUIDE OVERVIEW (DO NOT READ OUT LOUD TO CANDIDATE)

The purpose of this interview guide is to help you evaluate candidates. The questions shown here are drawn from a behavioral analysis of this position, conducted by you or a previous manager. Guidelines are suggested for evaluating the strength of candidates' answers.

We recommend you ask the questions *exactly as they are worded*. This is particularly important if multiple interviewers are interviewing 1 or more candidates (which we also recommend).

Please take notes in the space provided. *Write down what the candidate SAYS, rather than your impressions*. That will help you share the behavioral reasons for your conclusions and decision.

Remember to be as pleasant and friendly as you can be. You *can* deliver a demanding interview while also being polite and kind.

INTRODUCTORY STATEMENT

(PLEASE READ THIS OUT LOUD)

Thank you for interviewing with me today. Here at Manager Tools we use a behavioral interviewing style. I'll be asking a series of questions about experiences you've had and how you handled them. I've got a series of between 10 and 15 questions, and this might take us an hour, perhaps a little more time. Don't be surprised if others here ask you the same questions in other interviews - that's normal. We want to be sure that every person we hire has the same qualities that have made us so successful.

There will be times when I will ask you for more information, and don't worry, that's normal. I will be taking notes - please don't let it distract you. The way we'll do it is, first, I'll ask you some questions, and then I'll answer any questions you might have of me. When you're done with your questions, we'll finish up. I'm excited you're here - let's get started.

Tell me about yourself.

What behaviors to look for: Can they tell a coherent story of their experience? Does it makes sense with their resume? Can they articulate why they made certain decisions? How did those decisions turn out?

WEAK	STRONG
No coherent story.	A clear story, showing a path to this job.
Experience not articulated or not relevant.	Experience described, and attention drawn to the links to this job.
Unable to describe why they made decisions.	Reasoning is clear, even if the decision turned out poorly.

NOTES:

Question 1: Describe a situation when you have successfully managed multiple projects simultaneously.

What behaviors to look for: What planning or scheduling did they do to address the workload? Did they simply react to changes, or did they proactively stay on top of issues? Did they communicate reactively, or did they see this as normal professional responsibility and handle it well?

WEAK

Did not plan to address workload
Did not deliver projects on time or budget
Expresses dissatisfaction at having to manage
Did not delegate or coach others to achieve goals

STRONG

Has a clear method for managing multiple projects
Delivers projects on time and budget
Communicates regularly and methodically with others
Uses team's skills to ensure goals are met

NOTES:

Question 2: Tell me about your methods for following through on projects and details. How do you measure your success in this area?

What behaviors to look for: How complex was the project? How many details were there? Did they have a clear way of keeping track of the details? What was their approach to managing multiple, conflicting priorities and projects?

WEAK

Project is less complex than reasonable for this role

Details not proactively or methodically tracked

Does not have a method for managing conflicting priorities

Follows through only after aware of crises

STRONG

Project complexity is significant for this role

Follow through systems lead to improved performance

Systematic approach reduces errors and delays

Approach improves learning and future performance

NOTES:

Question 3: Tell me about a time when you have had to create and maintain detailed project plans and task lists. How did you go about this?

What behaviors to look for: How detailed were the plans? Were they electronic/efficient for use, or just kept on paper? Did others have access to them? Could they be used in the future? Did they have a way to improve on them over time?

WEAK

Details are less complex than reasonable for this role

Method of tracking not appropriate to project type or size

Detail could not be reused or accessed by others

Tracking does not create proactivity

STRONG

Project complexity equal/greater than required for role

Tracking method was appropriate to complexity

Tracking supports proactivity and improvement

Detail could be reused or used by others

Describes improvement mechanism

NOTES:

Question 4: Describe a situation when you noticed a particularly important detail and had to alert others to its importance.

What behaviors to look for: Did they react professionally? Did they over-react? What form did the communication take? Whom did they notify, and why those recipients? How did they discover the detail? Did they follow through?

WEAK	STRONG
Focused on wrong details	Saw the right details clearly
Failed to communicate in a timely way	Communicated in a way that highlighted the issue
Notified wrong people	Communicated with recipient in mind
Message not received well or correctly	Escalated communication appropriately if necessary

NOTES:

Question 5: Tell me about a time when you needed to follow instructions accurately. How did you ensure that your work was correct?

What behaviors to look for: What did the candidate do to ensure they understood the instructions? Did they write them down, or ask questions? What steps did they take to ensure that the work didn't get off track? Did they do anything to make sure the final product was what was expected?

WEAK

Did not remember instructions
Did not ask questions or clarify
Made errors left uncorrected
Had to be prompted with repeated guidance
Hid errors

STRONG

Took notes
Asked for clarification
Open with communications about questions and issues
Validated assumptions
Planned quality into the work
Checked work for accuracy

NOTES:

Question 6: Describe a situation when it's been necessary for you to create and maintain data accurately. What did you do to ensure the data began and remained accurate?

What behaviors to look for: Did they build a process to make sure errors were reduced? Or did they just "try to be careful." What steps did they take when changes were made or possible errors were identified?

WEAK	STRONG
No process	Built a clear process
Efforts were ad-hoc	Implemented process deliberately
Errors were systemic	Errors self-identified, corrected and communicated openly
Corrections were implemented case-by-case	Validated data and work with external sources
Denied responsibility for errors	Verbally owned process and outcomes.

NOTES:

Question 7: Tell me about a time where your communication with others—type, frequency, with whom, about what—helped you build rapport or create better relationships and outcomes?

What behaviors to look for: How did they learn about the other person? Were their exchanges based on respect, or simply getting an outcome? Did they continue the effort? Did they only do so to get a result, or do they show a pattern of always working at relationships?

WEAK	STRONG
Only interested in other person for potential outcome	Creates strategy for building relationships
Does not consistently build relationships	Articulates benefit of wide ranging relationships
Only calls when they want something	Gives before getting
Cannot demonstrate clear business benefit	Maintains relationships without near term business gain

NOTES:

Question 8: Tell me about an effective relationship you have created and kept over a long period. How did you achieve that?

What behaviors to look for: What do they describe as "long"? What actions did they take to keep the relationship active? Was there reciprocity – a willingness to share as well as benefit? What different forms of communication do they use? How do they communicate in ways that are helpful to the other person?

WEAK	STRONG
Long is less than 1-2 years	Has a strategy for maintaining relationship
Relies on other person to make contact	Gives without prospect of getting
Does not offer to give before getting	Communicates in multiple ways
Communicates in a limited way	Has relationships in different companies/industries
Has only internal relationships	Demonstrates different communication styles

NOTES:

Question 9: What tools do you use to ensure your communication is effective? Can you tell me about a time when one of them worked particularly well?

What behaviors to look for: What was their thought process for communicating? Do they communicate differently depending upon the content and the recipient? What did they do to customize their message for different people or situations?

WEAK

Only one or limited ways of communicating

No tailoring for audience

Lack of message planning

Singular delivery not flexible

Did not achieve planned objective

STRONG

Planned delivery carefully

Considered audience thoroughly

Rehearsed based on planning, message, and audience

Planning led to excellent outcome

Answers to questions tailored to audience member asking

NOTES:

Question 10: Describe a situation when you had to write something to persuade others.

What behaviors to look for: Did they structure their message based on the situation? Did they apply a standard template? How did they review and edit their work? Did they plan for time to review, or delay until time became a factor?

WEAK

Limited plan or structure to writing
Numerous errors in tone, spelling, grammar
Poor planning led to excess length
No clarity of goal
Excessive use of non-standard vocabulary

STRONG

Clear structure followed from message and objective
Edited carefully and repeatedly
Encouraged multiple inputs to help refine message
Considered audience and time in creation
Achieved objective

NOTES:

Custom Question 1: What's something you see about yourself as a potential weakness for this role?

WEAK   STRONG

NOTES:

Index

217